D0341262

Other Books by
DAVID REUBEN, M.D.

*Everything You Always Wanted to Know
About Sex—But Were Afraid to Ask*

Any Woman Can!

*How to Get More Out of Sex—
Than You Ever Thought You Could*

The Save-Your-Life Diet

THE
SAVE-YOUR-
LIFE-DIET
HIGH-FIBER
COOKBOOK

THE SAVE-YOUR-LIFE-DIET HIGH-FIBER COOKBOOK

David Reuben, M.D.
Barbara Reuben, M.S.

RANDOM HOUSE 🏠 NEW YORK

Copyright © 1975, 1976 by The Maleri Corporation

All rights reserved under International and
Pan-American Copyright Conventions.
Published in the United States by Random House, Inc., New York, and
simultaneously in Canada by Random House of
Canada Limited, Toronto.

Library of Congress Cataloging in Publication Data

Reuben, David R
The save-your-life-diet high-fiber cookbook.

1. High-fiber diet.   2. Cookery.   I. Reuben,
Barbara, joint author.   II. Title.
RM237.6.R39   641.5′63   76-14211
ISBN 0-394-40648-6

Manufactured in the United States of America

2 4 6 8 9 7 5 3

FIRST EDITION

*To my wife, Barbara, who has given me the only thing
of value in my life: her love*

*To my husband, David, with whom my life really
started and for whose unchanging love I live*

I would like to thank my good friend, agent, and comrade-in-arms, Don Congdon. He knows what I mean. I would also like to thank George Walsh, my editor and source of Irish enthusiasm —which blended well with my own Scottish stubbornness. Anne Tiffany helped everything to work—with her usual tact and grace.

I would like to thank Jim Wilcox of Random House for his expert assistance in editing the manuscript. Don Francisco Morelli helped taste-test the recipes. My appreciation also goes to Don Carlos Paniagua and Mayor Guillermo Vargas for making this book possible in many ways.

Our cook, Guadalupe Martinez, prepared the ingredients with enthusiasm and dedication. Stephanie Smirnow Adler tested recipes, and John Adler ate his way through them. Ann Habib and Gemila Habib contributed some superb Armenian delicacies. Karen deFigueres also tested recipes.

Our three children, David Junior, Cathy Nicole, and Amita, ate, laughed and, occasionally, spilled their way through this book. Everything here is more precious because of them.

CONTENTS

1

Food & Survival

The Save-Your-Life-Diet High-
Fiber Cookbook can literally save your life—and the lives of those
you love. In modern America we seem to have lost the instinct for
self-preservation. The war in Vietnam destroyed the lives of
40,000 citizens—immense social and political upheavals finally
brought it to a halt. Automobile crashes kill 55,000 Americans
every year—the government has spent billions of dollars to insti-
tute rigid controls over the manufacture and use of autos. Illegal
narcotics cause about 10,000 deaths a year—and billions are
spent on law enforcement and education. But in our society the
greatest single threat to survival for the average person is *breakfast,
lunch, and dinner.* Over one million Americans each year meet
an untimely death *directly as a result of the food they eat.* And
nobody seems to care. The undeniable facts are there for everyone to see. In the past seventy-five years—since the traditional
high-roughage diet has been replaced by the "modern" high
prestige low-roughage "convenience" diet—*new diseases* have
sprung up to devastate our society. Here is a small part of the
evidence:

Fatal heart attacks 1900: virtually unknown 1975: 750,000 *deaths*
Cancer of the colon 1900: insignificant incidence 1975: 99,000
  cases
Death from cancer of the colon 1900: insignificant 1975:
  49,000 *deaths*
Obesity 1900: relatively uncommon 1975: 100 million fat
  Americans (Remember, each pound of overweight after the
  age of forty means the loss of *one* year of life expectancy.)
Disabling Diverticulosis 1900: relatively rare disease 1975:
  Strikes *70* percent of all senior citizens

In the short span of seventy-five years, the diet of the average American has been converted from a useful source of nutrition for the human body to a plaything of giant food processors and advertising agencies. In effect, somebody stole our food while we weren't looking. For confirmation, consult your daily menu. The average citizen—man, woman, or child—starts off the day with "bread" that isn't bread at all.

Real bread is made from grains of wheat ground into flour, mixed with milk, yeast and salt, and baked in an oven.

The white puffy gloopy batter-whipped junk that clogs the intestines of our children is an *entirely different substance*. It is synthesized from what is left of the grain of wheat after everything worthwhile is removed—wheat germ, bran, and most of the vitamins and minerals. The starchy powder that remains is mixed with chemicals that no one in his right mind would swallow if he had a choice. That includes things like calcium bromate, sodium stearyl fumarate, and tricalcium phosphate, to name only a few. As a touching gesture, federal law requires bakers to add 5 hard-to-absorb synthetic vitamins to replace the 24 or so nutrients removed in the milling process.

The average American covers his slice of non-bread with imitation butter—euphemistically known as "margarine"—which is loaded with artificial coloring and flavoring. He washes the worthless combination down with an imitation orange drink (preferred by Astronauts), and may follow it with an imitation egg product "low in cholesterol." As he sips his chemically extracted instant coffee, dosed with refined sugar and "whitened" with a packet of chemicals innocently labeled "non-dairy creamer," this typical consumer flips through the morning paper. Perhaps he may even note the one-paragraph item on page 23: "CANCER DEATHS UP 6 PERCENT!"

In five minutes he has consumed no less than 48 powerful organic chemicals with names like diacetyl tartaric acid, butylated hyroxytoluene, sodium stearoyl-2-lactylate, polysorbate 60, azodicarbonamide, and at least 43 others. Without exception these chemicals have no valid role in human nutrition and are placed there *exclusively for the convenience of food manufacturers*. These additives allow them to store "convenience" foods up to a year without spoilage and help disguise the taste of inferior ingredients. (The claim that food additives lower the cost of food is unconvincing—as more and more chemicals have been added the cost of food has relentlessly increased.)

Even more frightening is the fact that 210 million Americans are unwilling experimental subjects in the testing of *known cancer-producing chemicals.* It works like this: The United States Food and Drug Administration—which is *supposed* to protect us from harmful chemicals in our daily diet—in conjunction with major food processors, made a decision worthy of a mentally retarded chimpanzee. It decided that *all chemicals added to food before 1958 must be safe because they had been in use before 1958!* That included thousands of untested chemicals, including the proven carcinogen cyclamate and poisonous BVO (brominated vegetable oil) used in fruit-flavored soft drinks. Other GRAS chemicals (*G*enerally *R*ecognized *A*s *S*afe) include monoisopropy citrate, propylene glycol, thiodipropionic acid, and glyceryl tri-acetate. The essential point is that these and other exotic non-food chemicals have been part of the human diet for fifty years or so at the most. In the identical fifty-year period the rate of all forms of cancer and heart disease has risen astronomically—this in itself should shed doubts on the safety of these additives. The irrational response of modern medicine has been to devise new and unbelievably expensive ways of prolonging the lives of victims of heart attacks and malignant tumors.

Literally tens of billions of dollars are spent each year on so-called "research" into new ways to kill and/or remove vital human tissue and organs affected by cancer. In contrast a few paltry millions are dispensed to discover how to *prevent* cancer.

Hundreds of responsible scientists and medical researchers agree on one undeniable point: the greatest single cause of cancer in America today is the methodical debasement of the basic elements of our diet. Over one million lives could be saved each year at *absolutely no cost* by simply leaving the natural roughage in our food and removing every artificial additive.

The gigantic companies that tinker with our daily diet—to their immense profit and our tragic loss—always disclaim responsibility in the same way. They insist that cancer and heart disease are caused by some mysterious force known as "stress." That's a handy way to look at things if you happen to be in the business of selling chemical-laden overprocessed food at grossly inflated prices. It is profitable to tell parents that the cancer their kids may grow into is caused by "the pressure and tension of modern life" instead of by the scientifically documented effect of the deadly chemicals in their food. In direct refutation of this foolishness are many studies separating the influence of diet and stress. The most fascinating is the revelation that Americans who are members of the religion known as Seventh-Day Adventists— and suffer the same stress as any other American, if not more— have much lower incidences of cancer and heart attacks. The major difference between ordinary Americans and Seventh-Day Adventist Americans is diet. SDA members consume a high-fiber diet by religious conviction and consume an extremely low level of food additives. Ordinary Americans, as is well known, consume low-fiber diets and eat, on the average, *twenty-two pounds* of artificial chemicals in their food each year.

As things stand in our free-enterprise society, no one is going to help you save your life—and the lives of your loved ones. The food processors tell you that low-fiber food dosed with chemical poisons make your food better. The FDA tells you that the food processors are right—and common sense tells you that your health and your life are being threatened with every bite you take. So, in the great American tradition, it's time to take things into your own hands. The menus and recipes and the philosophy of *The Save-Your-Life High-Fiber Cookbook* are designed to enable everyone to reproduce the diet that Americans consumed a hundred years ago—before 750,000 of us perished each year from heart attacks, before one of us succumbed to colon cancer every ten minutes by the clock, before seventy percent of those who collect Social Security also collect diverticulosis, before over half of us had our bodies bloated by ugly fat.

The scientific evidence is there in more than a thousand carefully validated research projects by internationally respected scientists. The incentive is there in the real opportunity to avoid agonizing disability and death. The means are there in the following pages of *The Save-Your-Life High-Fiber Cookbook*. The rest is up to you.

(Dr. and Mrs. Reuben will be happy to receive letters from readers sent in care of Random House, 201 East 50th Street, New York, N.Y. 10022.)

2

The Save-Your-Life Diet

T he process of digestion is one of the true miracles of the universe. Everything an individual consumes passes through about forty feet of complicated gastro-intestinal tubing and is acted upon by approximately two dozen chemical compounds. In the process such diverse dishes as frog's legs, calves' brains, oxtails, and pig's feet are converted to the basic building blocks of the human body. Briefly, this is the way the process works.

Once the food is chewed and swallowed, it passes into the stomach, where it is mixed with hydrochloric acid and digestive chemicals. It then passes into the small intestine—twenty-three feet of relatively small-diameter flexible pipe. Secretions from the liver are added, via the gall bladder, and other enzymes are secreted by the pancreas. By this time the food is well mashed and uniformly mixed with the digestive chemicals. Although some absorption may have occurred in the stomach, the major part of the nutrition is extracted from the food in the small intestine. Then the mushy mass of almost totally digested food is pushed into the colon. As far as most students of nutrition are concerned, that's when the game is over. As far as we are concerned, that's when things *really* get interesting.

For all too many years the five or so feet of the large intestine or colon were considered to be the sewage disposal plant of the body. The colon was viewed as a sort of septic tank to hold fecal material between bowel movements. As a result of many years of ingenious and sophisticated research it has now become obvious that the colon may play a vital role in the destiny of the human organism.

This is a summary of the basic principles of *The Save-Your-Life Diet* (Random House, 1975).

Instead of a stagnant holding tank, the colon is actually a living river. The dregs of digestion (feces is the plural of the Latin word *faex*, which means "dregs") are half liquid and half solid, and flow through the colon like an active stream. The solid portion of the fecal material precedes the liquid part, and the wall of the intestine selectively soaks up excess water.

For hundreds of years people have instinctively felt that there was something vaguely undesirable about allowing those dregs to accumulate day after day in that large flexible tunnel deep in the abdomen. Our grandparents prescribed "high enemas" or "colonic irrigations" to dispose of fecal accumulations. Even today there is a billion-dollar sale of laxatives designed to empty the colon of its contents. (An interesting fringe benefit of the extensive research on the effects of roughage showed the undesirability of taking laxatives for this purpose and even indicated that one type of commonly prescribed laxative can destroy the nerves that control the large intestine.) Without knowing why, our old-fashioned forebears were on the right track. One of the greatest risks a human being can take is to allow the remnants of his food—that is, the fecal end-products—to remain in contact with the lining of his colon for three and four days at a time. And that's exactly what 99 percent of Americans and others who eat a "modern" diet are doing. At the end of their digestive tract they are harboring a time bomb. This is what the researchers in laboratories around the world found.

Every cancer researcher agrees that cancer can be caused by body surfaces coming in contact with potent cancer-causing chemicals known as carcinogens. Unfortunately, there are examples all around us. Vinyl chloride as a cause of fatal cancer of the liver has gotten a great deal of publicity lately. Many of the food additives that have recently been banned are known or suspected to have caused cancer in human beings. The actual list of cancer-producing chemicals contains many hundreds of items, most of them organic chemicals with exotic names like methyl cholanthrene and the like.

In the process of studying cancer of the colon in rats, one investigator made a startling discovery. He fed a drug called cycasin to a group of normal rats. As expected, many of them promptly developed cancer of the colon. Then, on impulse, he tried the same experiment with a group of special rats who had been raised in such a way that their bodies were absolutely free of bacteria. To his amazement, none of the bacteria-free rats developed cancer. He then went on to analyze the urine and feces from both groups of rats, and what he found has life-and-death implications for two hundred million Americans. In the germ-free—and thus cancer-free—rats, the cancer-producing drug cycasin was recovered unchanged in the urine and feces. But in the cancer-ridden rats, only 35 percent of the chemical, at the most, was found in those waste products. That meant that the bacteria in the colon of the cancerous rats had broken down the cycasin into powerful, cancer-causing chemicals.

Turning their attention to human beings, scientists made a parallel and even more astonishing discovery. The human liver normally produces a chemical combination that we call *bile*. It is a thick greenish liquid essential for digestion, especially for the breakdown of fats. Bile is composed of several different chemicals known as bile acids that go by such arcane names as cholic acid and deoxycholic acid. (Incidentally, it is the pigments of bile that give feces their brownish color. If for some reason the liver is obstructed, as in hepatitis, bile cannot enter the small intestine and the bowel movement becomes pale, almost white, in color. The pigment may find its way into the skin and turn it greenish-yellow, causing jaundice.)

In any event, the investigators found that the average low-roughage-consuming American has two nutritionally significant types of bacteria in his colon; the dominant group is known as bacteroides and bifidobacteria. It has been proved beyond any doubt that the bile acid cholic acid can be converted into the powerful cancer-causing apcholic acid. Likewise the other bile acid, deoxycholic acid, can be changed into one of the most potent known carcinogens, 3-menthyl-cholanthrene.

The implications of those discoveries are simple and unequivocal: Americans who are on lifelong low-roughage diets are probably converting their own harmless bile acids into awesome cancer-producing compounds within the confines of their own large intestines.

Further proof lies in the fact that individuals on low-roughage diets pass decreased amounts of bile acids in their bowel movements, indicating that, like cancerous rats, they have broken them down into carcinogenic compounds. On the other hand, those persons who consume high-roughage diets have a colon dominated by streptococcus and lactobacillus bacteria, which do not appear to attack the bile acids and break them down. As additional confirmation of this protection, individuals on high-roughage diets pass a much greater proportion of intact, unchanged bile acids in their feces. Assuming that these potentially lethal chemicals are accumulating in the colon as each day passes, the body's next line of defense is to get them out of contact with the soft and vulnerable lining of the large intestine. Ironically, only those on high-roughage diets—who are never exposed to the cancer chemicals—don't have to worry on that score. They store their freshest fecal products in the colon for less than eighteen hours on the average, based on the fact that special markers pass through their *entire* digestive tracts in about twenty-four hours.

The low-roughage carcinogen-producing American diet allows the fecal mass and its store of cancer chemicals to wash over the colon for seventy-two hours or longer—and in the case of some British patients, for as long as two weeks. Even our valuable and dedicated astronauts are deliberately fed a special low-roughage diet which delays their bowel movements as long as six days. (Cancer of the colon seems a high price to pay for the exploration of space.)

Beyond that, each bowel movement consists of 20 to 30 percent bacteria—so the faster any bile-acid-splitting bacteria are moved out of the intestine, the less mischief they can perform.

Other experiments leave little doubt that encouraging prolonged contact between the remnants of digestion and the wall of the colon is inviting disaster. In those experimental animals who are deliberately given cancer, simply isolating a loop of intestine so that feces never flow over it prevents malignant changes in that isolated loop. There is a further fascinating observation made by a leading researcher: For all practical purposes, only two epithelial-lined body channels are common sites of cancer—the bronchial tubes, which are the location of the most common form of lung cancer, and the colon. These are—not by coincidence —the only channels or tubes that are exposed to foreign substances. The bronchial tubes are exposed to cigarette smoke and the colon is exposed to the slow-moving stream containing residual carcinogenic chemicals from unnaturally low-roughage foods.

The irony of being an unwilling accomplice in the development of one's own colon cancer is compounded by the fact that modern therapy for cancer of that organ is not really encouraging. In fact, it has not basically changed since 1900. The strategy is to wait helplessly until the cancer is firmly established within your large intestine. You will know the time has arrived when you have pain, bleeding, diarrhea, or constipation. Then, as the cancer is growing day by day, medical science finally makes a dedicated and valiant effort to save your life.

The actual treatment of the malignant tumor is based on destroying the affected part of the organ as well as a sizable amount of healthy tissue. In many cases of cancer of the colon (and the extension of the colon, the rectum), that means closing off the anus and repositioning it permanently in the abdominal wall. In some cases, tumor tissue (and an unavoidable amount of normal tissue) is destroyed by radiation—similar to the fallout from a nuclear explosion. Patients are also treated on occasion by chemotherapy—that is, the administration of extremely toxic drugs designed to kill tumor cells without damaging the patient's body permanently. Tragically, in spite of the Herculean efforts of devoted specialists, barely half of those stricken with colon cancer survive. How much better it would be to simply add roughage to one's diet and drastically reduce the risk of ever succumbing to colon cancer.

Unfortunately, the risk for Americans is a very real one. The United States has nearly the highest rate of colon cancer in the world. About 42 out of every 100,000 American men between the ages of thirty-five and sixty-four develop cancer of the colon and rectum. In some areas of the country the risk is even greater. For example, in the state of Connecticut, the rate is 52 per 100,000, and the state of New York has a rate of 46 per 100,000. It seems more than a coincidence that our national diet is nearly the lowest in roughage of any nation in the world. By contrast, the incidence of colon cancer in the United States is 900 percent greater than that of Nigeria and 1,300 percent greater than Uganda, two countries with traditional high-roughage diets.

Although rural African blacks are protected from cancer of

the colon by their high-roughage diet, that immunity does not extend to their American cousins. After two generations of living in the United States and gradually shifting to a low-fiber diet, the rate for colon cancer among black Americans is almost identical to that of their white fellow citizens. That's exactly what one would expect, since both black and white digestive systems now operate in deadly slow motion. The same misfortune has befallen second-generation Japanese who have moved to Hawaii and the U.S. and forsaken the traditional Japanese high-fiber diet. The rate of colon malignancy is also rising among those who dwell in Japan but have made the transition to low-roughage foods.

As far as cancer of the colon is concerned, it seems that more than enough of the evidence is in to implicate the modern low-fiber diet.

That's the bad news. But the good news is that cancer of the colon—and rectum—is a potentially *preventable* disease. And the most likely way to prevent it is simply to restore the human diet to what it should be, to what it used to be, before cancer of the large intestine killed and crippled so many victims every year. Remember, the longer we delay changing our diet the greater the chance that it will be too late. The same holds true—perhaps even in a more immediate sense—when it comes to heart attacks.

There are several ways of restoring adequate dietary fiber to our daily diets. First, we might switch to the staple menu of rural Africans and Asians. That means ground corn, boiled bananas, freshly dug potatoes, and plenty of beans. Most Americans would be understandably reluctant to make that kind of substitution.

But there is another possibility: we can adapt the modern American diet so that it prolongs our lives—and the lives of our children—instead of shortening them. We can thread our way through the maze of potentially lethal fresh-from-the-factory simulated foods and eat the way human beings were designed to eat. We can nourish our bodies the way men and women nourished theirs for 50,000 years—before heart attacks, colon cancer, diabetes, and all the other degenerative diseases that we take for granted felled millions of innocent victims.

We can make the little sacrifices that can protect us from the suffering and death implicit in cancer of the colon, heart attacks, diabetes, and all the other degenerative diseases that suddenly erupted with the advent of the low-fiber "modern" diet.

When I wrote *The Save-Your-Life Diet,* early in 1975, I was concerned that Americans might lack the courage to make the necessary changes to literally "save their lives." At that time, I wrote: "Ninety-nine percent of American families will reject that regimen, since they have been conditioned to the 'fashionable' and seductive low-roughage routine."

It didn't turn out that way. Since then I have received many thousands of letters saying, in effect:

"Doctor, I'm ready, my family is ready. We eat the bran, we feel better, but instead of *supplementing* our low-fiber diet, we want to, once and for all, eat the way we were designed to eat."

I was also concerned about the cost of converting to an authentic high-fiber diet. My readers clarified that for me as well:

"My husband and I talked it over and decided that the health and well-being of our family were more important than saving money on food. So we started on the traditional high-fiber diet— *and kept careful records of our expenses.* We were amazed to find at the end of the month that our food costs were actually lower on the high-fiber diet!

"It worked out this way: fruit and vegetable costs were higher since we only bought fresh produce. But since canned and frozen foods have gone up so much, we spent only about 10 percent more than we had been spending in that area. We bought more fresh whole grains but far less meat. And we stopped buying so-called 'convenience' foods altogether. I just couldn't find whole-grain cake mixes and high-fiber frozen dinners. When I did the final calculations, I was amazed to discover that our total food costs for the month went down about 15 percent!

"If I didn't have the cash register receipts right in front of me, I wouldn't have believed that it was possible to buy more food—*real food*—and spend less money."

Our goal is to increase the amount of dietary fiber in our daily diet to *approach* the African-Asian-Latin American ideal of about twenty-four grams (roughly three-quarters of an ounce) a day. The simplest and most effective way to accomplish that is to convert to a high-fiber diet program.

There is an almost infallible way to tell when the ideal amount of bran is being consumed. When the bowel movement is large in amount, well-formed, low in odor, and passed without straining once (or twice) a day, the roughage in the diet is just right. For the first week or so, there should be an increase in the amount of gas passed, and there may also be a feeling of fullness after consuming the bran. Those are two important signs that the extra fiber is doing its job.

If there is any difficulty passing the bowel movement, the bran may be used as a supplement, in small amounts. Someone who is eating a natural high-fiber diet might add two teaspoons morning and night for three days or so, and judge the results according to the effect on bowel function. Remember that the digestive system that has been crippled so long on a low roughage diet needs a reasonable amount of time to adjust to the new and more natural way of eating.

The diameter of the large intestine increases, the food and products of digestion flow through the digestive system faster, less cholesterol is produced by the liver, and the whole pace of digestion quickens.

Your gastrointestinal system will begin to function normally for the first time in your life. When you consume a high roughage diet the following changes should take place:

1. The bacteria in your colon will shift to the lactobacillustreptococcus forms, which encourage normal fermentation of the food that you consume, rather than the abnormal fermentation of the low-roughage diet.
2. The amount of fat and fatty acid that you excrete in your bowel movement should increase significantly.
3. The rate of absorption of the food that you consume should decline.
4. The level of lipids (fat) in your blood should diminish.

Within the first seven days you will begin to enjoy the benefits of having restored the essential roughage to your diet. Constipation will vanish, almost without exception. Those who suffered from hemorrhoids or other anal/rectal problems may find relief. Victims of diverticulosis—after obtaining their doctor's consent to add roughage—should feel an almost immediate improvement. Those with elevated cholesterol levels may want to have their blood cholesterol checked just before they use bran to correct their roughage deficiency, and then have their doctors repeat the test in six weeks. The results should be gratifying and reassuring for both doctor and patient.

Although no diet in the world is going to reverse the physical changes that are evident in varicose veins, when a person no longer has to strain with each bowel movement, the tremendous pressure that such straining generates is absent, and the damaged veins can function much better. At the same time, further vein damage is prevented.

Another bonus comes in the battle against obesity. Bran can be included in nearly every weight-reduction diet—with your doctor's approval, as usual. Being able to eat something three times a day that is chewable, has body, and provides a feeling of fullness—without significant calories—is a dieter's dream come true. We'll examine a high-roughage reducing diet a little further on.

The last benefit of a high-roughage diet is difficult to explain. It is a kind of an indescribable feeling of well-being, the realization that finally, after many years, your body is functioning the way it was designed to function. People who have followed the diet characterize that sensation as "feeling like a machine that's humming along," or "alert and energetic the way I was twenty years ago," or simply "alive again." When you experience the sensation, you'll understand.

An important question is "How long should I stay on the high-roughage diet?" The best answer: Only as long as you want to feel good. As you notice your appetite for semisynthetic junk food beginning to wane and your appreciation of wholesome food beginning to increase, the high-fiber diet will become a way of life. Actually this question answers itself, because after a month on a normal high-fiber diet, there will be no way that you can be convinced to go back to the unappealing low-roughage way of life.

Try it and you'll see.

3
Basic Principles of High-Fiber Cooking

For centuries there have been three basic elements to successful cooking: science, art, and health.

The scientific aspect of cooking has been relatively straightforward. It consists of applying heat and cold, stirring and mixing, and adding natural emulsifiers like eggs, natural binders like oil, and doing all the rest of the things necessary to change the structure of basic ingredients.

The art of cooking consists of doing the scientific things in such a way that the final product is fit to eat. It requires a subtle blending of textures, flavors, shapes and sizes, and even colors, to please the five senses. (Yes, even the sense of hearing. What would celery and popcorn be without the crunch?)

The role of *health* in cooking *except for the last forty years or so in the United States* has been self-regulating. Human beings, offered a reasonable selection of food, will naturally choose a balanced diet. This has been proved over and over again in so-called "cafeteria" experiments. In these fascinating studies, controlled groups such as children in orphanages, prisoners, are offered the free choice of a wide variety of foods. For example, a large buffet is set out at each meal, including meat, desserts, vegetables, fruits, bread products, candy, etc. Dietitians, usually hidden from view, keep careful record of what each individual consumes. While the short-term results are often bizarre—children may eat only desserts for a day or so—when the total consumption is analyzed over a week or a month, each individual diet is almost always found to be completely balanced. Left alone, the human organism has the ability to select its own perfectly balanced diet. Almost everyone has had similar experiences in the form of a sudden "craving" for an orange, an apple, a piece of meat, or something similar. That's the reason serious vitamin deficiencies are nearly impossible in healthy people consuming unprocessed food.

For example, primary beri-beri, a potentially fatal disease, is found only among communities which consume large quantities of white rice. It is a disease inflicted on innocent eaters by food processors. Scurvy, which affected British and American sailors in the days of sailing vessels, was the result of stupidity and dietary fads more than anything else; previous generations of sailors from the Vikings to the Venetians had little trouble with the disease. But salted meat and hardtack are poor sources of vitamin C. If the sailors had opted for a little red pepper, garlic or chili on their beef, or even enjoyed boiled lima beans, they would have been scurvy-free. The myth of lime juice or orange juice as a source of vitamin C still lingers on. (As a matter of scientific fact, sweet bell peppers contain three times the vitamin C of citrus fruits, and at much lower cost.)

Nutritional diseases only become manifest when the human diet is artificially manipulated. Until recently, that was the result of wars, famines, and plagues. Nowadays it is the result of a desire to consume cottony white-flour Wonder "bread," chemical-laden Cool Whip, Tang, margarine, Pringles' idea of potato chips, and the hundreds of other factory-made foods. The demand for these immensely profitable concoctions must be created by the intense mind-manipulation that bombards millions of defenseless people thousands of times a day via television, radio, magazines, newspapers, billboards, and even skywriting. Sophisticated appeals to a wife's insecurity, a husband's desire for status, and a small child's fear that he will not grow are used to peddle products that do not fulfill the nutritional needs of our people, and often contain poisonous, disease-producing substances. The grim truth is that the wives and mothers of America, as well as their husbands and children, have been abandoned by their government. The FDA and FTC, the Congress, the elected leaders, and even the courts allow food processors to distort the basic necessities of human nutrition beyond all belief—in the name of profit.

We only have one defense against the fabulously wealthy and

powerful food companies: *we don't have to eat what they tell us to eat!* We can say appropriately, in the words of Madison Avenue, "Please, Mother, I'll do it myself." And this is how we can do it.

The original concept of *The Save-Your-Life-Diet High-Fiber Cookbook* was to answer the requests of the readers of *The Save-Your-Life Diet.* One quarter million copies of that book were sold in hardcover, and literally thousands of men and women wrote asking for a selection of recipes that would enable them to restore the missing fiber to their diet. So my wife, Barbara, and I set out to compile and create—often from scratch—the tastiest and most satisfying high-fiber dishes possible. We vowed to produce a collection of recipes that went far beyond just "adding bran to everything," and we resisted the offers of our friends of "Grandmother's favorite bran muffin recipe." Let's face it, bran is not a gourmet's delight. It is simply an inexpensive concentrated source of roughage to supplement our modern lethal diet.

The goal of *The Save-Your-Life-Diet High-Fiber Cookbook* is to offer an entirely *new* and entirely *old* way of eating food which is as close as possible to the way God provided it and as far as possible from the hazardous concoctions of the food processors.

Something predictable happened in the process. It became obvious that it wasn't rational to offer fiber-restored recipes which contained artificial coloring, artificial flavoring, imitation butter (margarine), MSG, and all the rest. Therefore the ingredients and the cooking methods are as close to natural as reasonably possible. (In this context, "natural" means unprocessed.) It would be wonderful to use only what we raise in our own gardens, free from dangerous pesticides, harmful types of fertilizer, and synthetic growth hormones. (Incidentally, everyone who can raise their own food—or any part of it—*should.*) But as a practical matter, the least we can settle for is that every ingredient in our daily diet should be untouched by chemicals, milling, artificial coloring, de-vitaminization, destruction by heat, and any other form of tampering. The closer we can come to this ideal, the better will be the result.

The following list describes some of the foods that are used in *The Save-Your-Life-Diet High-Fiber Cookbook,* along with the reasons we use them. There are also some foods that we *don't* use—along with the reasons for *not* using them:

1. Flour: 100 percent stone-ground whole-wheat flour or 100 percent whole-wheat pastry flour or flour with germ intact.

2. Whole-meal corn meal.

3. Milk: Whole milk, unhomogenized if possible. Homogenized milk costs more, conceals the fact that most of the cream has been extracted to be sold back to you at an inflated price, and may cause abnormal elevation of blood fats. (There are some interesting scientific studies that suggest homogenized milk, with its very small fat particles, may overload the bloodstream with larger than normal amounts of fat.)

4. Butter: Sweet butter made from sweet cream is far superior to imitation butter known as "margarine."

5. Fruits and Vegetables: First-quality fresh fruits and vegetables are most desirable from the standpoint of taste and nutrition. Wash them well—some supermarkets give the already-pesticide-soaked produce another spraying when it is delivered to the store! There is one important exception—for those who are really pressed for time, the quick and easy and super-instant versions must take advantage of dried, canned, and frozen produce. Obviously this is a slight deviation from the ideal, but it's better than the old low-fiber way.

6. Cooking Oil: A difficult situation that requires a bit of explanation. Since one principle is to restrict our diet to foods that have been in use for at least a thousand years or so—to eliminate the chance of encountering some unsuspected lethal quality—the whole question of cooking oils takes a little thought. The well-accepted and proven-harmless oils have been used since Biblical times—and before—with no proven ill effects.

But things are changing. Vast amounts of peanut oil now are made from old and moldy peanuts contaminated with a substance called "aflatozin," one of the most powerful cancer-causing substances known. Many harmless oils are now doped up with butylated hydroxyloluene or butylated hydroxyanisole (disguised on the label as innocent-sounding "BHT" or "BHA"), silicones, and other powerful organic chemicals that don't belong in anyone's diet.

Many "seed" oils like cottonseed are relatively new, and their long-term effects on human health are not known. Corn and olive oil are good choices, as well as sesame and soybean oil.

Small amounts of butter and whole milk are used for their flavor in the recipes that follow. If used as part of a high-fiber diet, they can be considered nutritious additions to the diet.

Incidentally, more and more nutritional scientists—especially those who do not receive grants from the major food processors— are becoming alarmed at the radical and unjustified changes that the "cholesterol phobia" is producing in the modern American diet.

Ironically, the misinterpretation of a few key medical articles, plus the chance to extract hundreds of millions of dollars from frightened families, has produced a dangerous distortion of the American diet.

This is the way it happened:

Back in 1924 some medical researchers found that by feeding *rabbits* a high-cholesterol diet, they were able to produce deposits of a fatty substance in the animals' blood vessels. Rationally, that information should have been of interest only to rabbits. However, other researchers observed that human beings also developed a similar fatty substance. It was also obvious that humans consumed a certain amount of cholesterol in their diets. Specifically, animal fats, meat, milk products, and eggs contain substantial amounts of cholesterol!

The next step was mass hysteria: "Don't eat cholesterol! You'll get a heart attack!" became a battle cry. Dozens of articles appeared in popular magazines listing cholesterol-containing foods and warning readers away from them. With their usual lightning response, food processors rushed to market with at least 200 products guaranteed to lower the cholesterol *intake (but not the blood cholesterol level)* of gullible consumers. In the anticholesterol panic, a major drug manufacturer marketed a capsule guaranteed to lower blood cholesterol. (It did that—at the same time at caused baldness, blindness, and loss of sexual desire.)

But in the mass hysteria—intensified by food-processor scare-advertising—these important scientific facts were overlooked:

1. In human beings, *there is no precise proven connection between cholesterol intake and fatty deposits in the arteries.*
2. The cholesterol you eat is only one source of that substance in your body. Most tissues of the body manufacture cholesterol, and the liver is the main producer. In fact, *the less cholesterol you eat, the more your liver makes on its own.*
3. Most of the associations between high cholesterol intake and heart attacks have been observed in nations like the United States and England—where the diet is a *low-fiber diet.*
4. There is conclusive evidence that persons on a high-fiber diet can consume a high-fat, high-cholesterol diet and still maintain a normal blood fat and blood cholesterol level.

In a recent attempt to prove "once and for all" that low-cholesterol intake reduces the incidence of heart attacks, a large group of American men were placed on a low-cholesterol diet. After an extended period of time they showed a marginally lower incidence of heart attacks—and increased incidence of cancer! Their diet, not by coincidence, was also a *low-fiber diet.*

A careful reading of the authoritative scientific literature provides ample evidence that the dietary intake of cholesterol is not necessarily an important factor in heart attacks. Here are some of the most important articles on the subject:

Gould, G., *Am. J. Med.*, 11:209, 1951.
Heymann, W., and Rack, F., *Am. J. Dis. Childh.*, 65:235, 1943.
Karinen et al., *J. App. Physiol.*, 11:143, 1957.
Ladd, A. T., et al., *Fed. Proc.*, 8:360, 1949.
Sperling, G., et al., *J. Nutr.*, 55:399, 1955.
Splitter, S. D., *Metabolism*, 17:1129, 1968.

The "low-cholesterol fad" is important in relation to *The Save-Your-Life-Diet High-Fiber Cookbook*. It works this way:
The entire human race may be considered part of an extended nutritional experiment.
If substantial numbers of men and women consume foods which are harmful or unhealthy, the increase in sickness and death soon becomes apparent. Some interesting examples are the fava bean, consumed by Italians, which can cause serious poisoning, chronic

ergot poisoning of Russian peasants who consumed damaged rye, and the presumed chronic illness of ancient Roman aristocrats, resulting from the use of lead food utensils—and the consequent lead poisoning.

The so-called low-cholesterol substitute foods, in general, are new to nutrition, and their long-term hazards are unknown. For example, human beings have been eating butter for over 3000 years with no ill effects. Imitation butter (called "margarine") has only been consumed in large quantities over the past thirty years. Olive oil has been in use since Biblical times. Cottonseed oil is a relatively new product, produced from the waste of the cotton-ginning process. Eggs have been consumed by humans for a million years—long before heart attacks began to decimate the human race. Imitation eggs, made from egg whites, milk products, soybean oil, and synthetic vitamins, are now being tested on millions of guinea pigs who pay the full retail price. The question really boils down to this:

Isn't it a wonderful and profitable coincidence that the most popular medical theories of the moment require us to abandon the natural diet of the human race and consume newly created and very expensive factory foods?

But if you really want something to think about, ponder this: The same gigantic complex of food processors that sells you "cholesterol-reducing" food products at high prices is clandestinely slipping you "cholesterol-producing" foods—also at very high prices.

It's absurdly simple. According to the "cholesterol theory," certain cooking oils discourage the formation of cholesterol. These include sunflower oil, safflower oil, corn oil, and a few others. These are the high-priced "polyunsaturated" products that play on the fears of the masses. The same companies feed the unsuspecting consumer massive doses of the one cooking oil which is considered (according to the theory) most likely to increase cholesterol! That oil is *coconut oil*, the cheapest and potentially most hazardous (according to the companies that sell it to you) oil of all, since it is lowest in "polyunsaturates." But you will rarely see the name "coconut oil" on a label. They simply say "vegetable oil," because your elected representatives in Washington let them put that little trick over on you. (Federal law does *not* require the exact name of the oil to be stated on the label.) Commercial salad dressing, potato chips, imitation whipped cream, coffee "whitener," many margarines, snack crackers, many commercial cookies and pastries, candies, and virtually every other mass-market food product made with oil is dripping with coconut oil or its brother, "palm kernel" oil. Millions of unsuspecting men and women obediently pass up wholesome butter and eggs—"to keep the cholesterol down"—while they are secretly dosed with cheap, presumably "cholesterol-producing," coconut oil.

Now to some technical details.

We recommend that you use cast-iron cookware (unenameled) in preparing these dishes. First of all, it is magnificently ugly. Secondly, and more important, it adds—at no cost—a significant amount of iron to your diet. (Some of the iron from the pot goes into the food as it cooks.) Thirdly, cast-iron heats evenly and lasts forever.

You will notice that no salt is added to these recipes—except for what is already in the ingredients. Some ingredients, like bouillon cubes and commercial broth, do contain large amounts of salt—just take that into consideration. You can add the amount of salt you want—remembering that excessive amounts of salt are associated with high blood pressure.

As far as sugar is concerned, we suggest only honey, molasses, and *real* raw sugar. Regrettably, genuine raw sugar is not available in the United States, unless you want to make your own from sugar eets or sugar cane. Reconstructed raw sugar is better than white sugar, and if you have no other choice, brown sugar is better—by a hair—than white sugar.

We can see no reason for eating saccharin or any other chemical compound to simulate sweetness.

As each day goes by, more and more of the natural (unprocessed) foods can be found in your local markets. But don't hesitate to pick up the hard-to-find items in the health food store. The money will be well spent.

Which brings us to the most important point of all—the nature of food in relation to the human body. Your body is nothing more nor less than a collection of billions of tiny cells, organized into various specialized tissues and organs. Each of these microscopic structures requires a constant supply of amino acids, chemicals

4

Grains:
Forgotten Friends

Some years ago a wealthy Italian was in Scotland on a short business trip. The first morning he asked the waiter to bring him a "typical Scottish breakfast." When the first course, a steaming bowl of oatmeal, was placed before him, he wrinkled his nose in displeasure and pushed it away.

"Do you expect a *man* to eat that?" he growled. "In Italy, we feed *that* to the horses!"

"Aye," agreed the waiter. "That's why Italy has the finest horses and Scotland has the finest men."

Without getting into the details of the Scottish-Italian debate that followed, the truth is that over the past fifty years American horses, cows, pigs, sheep, and goats have been eating better than American boys and girls—and their parents. Virtually the only grain products available for mass consumption have been over-processed rice and tasteless cooked cereals.

The entire category of natural grains was driven into exile many years ago when the following four myths were created—by "experts" who should have known better:

1. "Starchy foods like rice are fattening."
They most emphatically are not fattening—when served in their high-fiber form and included as part of the high-fiber diet.

2. "Whole grains take too long to cook."
When considered as part of total meal preparation, high-fiber grain products require no more effort than their expensive nutritionally inferior low-fiber counterparts.

Let's say it takes thirty-five minutes to prepare dinner, including setting the table, unwrapping the food, washing, peeling, chopping, mixing, frying, boiling, etc. Under those circumstances, cooking high-fiber brown rice (thirty minutes) requires the *same total effort* as boiling low-fiber "instant" white rice in ten minutes, since the rice itself cannot be served until the entire meal is ready.

3. "Most Americans don't really go for rice and all that other exotic stuff—just give 'em meat and potatoes!"
Most Americans have never even tasted natural high-fiber rice— much less the rich array of other high-fiber grains that other nations take for granted as part of their main dishes.

Just giving them "meat and potatoes" has also just given them the world's highest rate of heart attack, cancer of the colon, and other dubious medical distinctions.

The truth is that whole grains can stand by themselves in anyone's menu planning. Besides being high in fiber, they have these outstanding advantages:

1. They are more nutritious, since they contain the full dose of natural vitamins, minerals, and trace elements. In effect, they retain nearly everything they were "born with." How senseless it is to take a grain of brown rice, expend money and effort to remove essential vitamins and minerals, and then spend more to *partially and incompletely* replace the wasted substance with synthetic vitamins!

2. Whole grains are more satisfying than their overprocessed counterparts, since they have not been robbed of a long list of vital elements in the refining process. A mouthful of whole-grain rice offers much more to the body than a mouthful of overprocessed starchy white rice—and the body knows it.

3. Whole grains are *much less fattening* than the equivalent low-fiber product. Their high-fiber content requires more chewing, takes up moisture from the digestive system—thereby giving a feeling of fullness—and tends to slow absorption of calories in the small intestine.

4. They cost less. *Someone* has to pay for all those big mills that strip the fiber and nutrition from natural grains. Someone has to pay for the millions of dollars in advertising and the fancy packaging. Someone has to pay for the synthetic chemicals that are used to partially "enrich" or "fortify" the de-nutrified commercial versions. Someone has to pay for the massive amounts of fuel consumed in overprocessing. Guess who pays?

There is another facet to the lower cost of using whole grains. Natural-grain dishes—because of their richness and nutritional value—tend to lower the consumption of ultra-expensive meat and meat products. If each person in a family of four cuts his consumption of meat by only four ounces a day at a time when meat costs $2 a pound, the savings in food cost will be exactly $2 a day, or about $60 a month. That program should easily provide more than enough protein in the diet, pay for the equivalent in delicious high-fiber foods, lower the amount of fat which the body must process, and still offer savings at the end of the month to pay for some extra little luxuries for everyone.

When it comes to grains, most of us have led sheltered lives. White rice at Chinese restaurants, "wild" rice (which isn't rice at all) rarely on holidays, and cooked cereals made from wheat or rice or oats when Mother decided the weather was cold enough. Those of us with Jewish, Armenian, or Middle Eastern friends had occasional exposures to "exotic" grain products, and some Southerners can remember when grits were really grits—not pure white blobs of grainy instant library paste. Let's take a look at some of the exciting and appetizing possibilities. First, there is cracked wheat.

Known among the Armenians as "bulghur," among the Turks as "bulgur," and Arab peoples as "burghul," cracked wheat is simply cereal wheat that has had each grain "cracked" into four or five little pieces. It contains every element of the whole wheat berry, and has a *crude fiber* content of about 69 grams per ounce. Anyone who enjoys whole-wheat bread, bran muffins, or a wholesome "wheaty" flavor in any form will wonder how they could have lived all these years without cracked wheat.

Recipes

A good recipe to start with is: Basic Cracked Wheat, which contains three times the protein and twice the fiber of mashed potatoes and, many people think, ten times the taste.

Basic Cracked Wheat—Traditional

Cook 2 cups cracked wheat in:
1 tbsp. butter
1 medium onion, chopped
4 cups beef **or** *chicken stock*

Add to cracked wheat:
2 tbsp. butter
2 medium onions, chopped
1 medium green pepper, chopped
3 cloves garlic, minced
2 medium tomatoes, chopped
1 tsp. crushed dried oregano
1 tbsp. crushed dried mint **or** *¼ cup fresh chopped mint*
Freshly ground black pepper to taste (¼ tsp.)
Yogurt
More mint to sprinkle on top if desired

In a 2–2½-quart saucepan melt 1 tablespoon butter and sauté one of the onions, chopped, until transparent. Add chicken or beef broth and bring to a boil. Add cracked wheat, bring to a boil again, reduce heat to very low, cover, and simmer for 20 minutes.

In a frying pan sauté the remaining chopped onions, green pepper, and garlic in the remaining butter until onions are transparent. Add tomatoes, oregano, mint, and black pepper. Sauté another minute or two.

When the cracked wheat is cooked, toss it with onion and tomato mixture. Serve topped with dollops of yogurt and more mint sprinkled on top. The mint is an important flavor in this recipe. Serves 6.

Quick and Easy (SERVING TIME: 10 MINUTES)
Prepare cracked wheat ahead of time by cooking it in broth for 20 minutes. At dinnertime you have only to do the following: Sauté in 2 tablespoons butter: 2 medium onions, chopped, and 1 medium green pepper, chopped, with 3 cloves of garlic, minced. When onions become transparent, add 2 medium chopped tomatoes, 1 teaspoon crushed oregano and 1 tablespoon crushed mint and freshly ground black pepper. Sauté another minute or two, mix with the cooked cracked wheat and heat. Serve hot with dollops of yogurt and more mint sprinkled on top.

Super-Instant
Super-Instant is really nothing more than good planning. Take the cracked-wheat recipe above, for example. The vegetable preparation time is 5 minutes at most. If you cook the cracked wheat the *night before* you serve it, all you have to do is warm it up and add the vegetables at dinnertime. That gives you good natural food with less preparation time *and much lower cost* than the usual overprocessed low-fiber and overpromoted junk food.

You'll notice that each recipe shows a "serving time." That means the actual time devoted to preparation of the dish. It does not include "processing time," such as baking for 40 minutes, simmering on the back of the stove for an hour, and the like. For example, when you're baking your own Instant High-Fiber Breakfast Cakes for 40 minutes in the oven, you don't have to stand there watching them. You can read a book, talk to your friends on the phone, take a nap, or even go out to the store. If you think of it in those terms, high-fiber cooking can be faster than the unhealthy old-fashioned low-fiber system of cooking. One other thing—don't worry about partially cooking something the night before and then heating it up the following day—as in some of the "Super-Instant" recipes. Generally, the flavor improves overnight, the food values are unimpaired, and as long as you refrigerate it, it will be even better the next day.

Super-Instant Version of Basic Cracked Wheat
(SERVING TIME: 5 MINUTES)
Prepare the cracked wheat ahead of time by cooking the cracked wheat in broth for 20 minutes. At dinnertime:

1 8-ounce can tomato sauce	1 tsp. ground or crushed
1 tsp. powdered garlic	oregano
2 tbsps. dehydrated onions	1 tbsp. mint flakes
2 tbsps. dehydrated green	
pepper	

Pour the tomato sauce into a saucepan. Add the spices, mix in the cracked wheat, already cooked, heat well, and serve with yogurt and mint as before.

Bran Supplement: Add ¾ cup bran to cracked wheat if desired. But be sure to add ¼ cup water to cooking liquid if you supplement with bran.

🦃🦃

Bulghur, Armenian style, has even more fiber and more flavor than the traditional version.

Cracked Wheat, Armenian Style—Traditional

SERVING TIME: 20 MINUTES

For cracked wheat:	*Add to cooked cracked wheat:*
1 tbsp. butter **or** oil	2 tbsps. butter **or** oil
1 chopped onion	½ cup slivered or chopped
4 cups beef **or** chicken stock	almonds **or** whole pignolia
2 cups cracked wheat	nuts
Freshly ground pepper to taste	¼ cup raisins **or** currants
(½ tsp.)	¼ cup chopped dates
	1 tsp. allspice
	1 tsp. cinnamon
	1 tbsp. honey

In a 2–2½-quart saucepan sauté onion in 1 tablespoon butter or oil until transparent. Add the broth and bring to a boil. Add cracked wheat and pepper to taste. When it boils again, lower heat, and simmer 20 minutes. In a frying pan sauté the nuts, raisins, dates, and spices in remaining butter or oil. After 2 minutes add a tablespoon honey. Mix well. Set aside. When cracked wheat is cooked, toss nut mixture with cracked wheat and serve. Serves 6.

Quick and Easy (SERVING TIME: 10 MINUTES)
Cook cracked wheat the night before (while you're watching TV, for example). Then at dinnertime, sauté the nut-raisin-date mixture, mix in with the cracked wheat and heat.

Super-Instant (SERVING TIME: 5 MINUTES)
Cook the cracked wheat the night before, but for only 15 minutes. Refrigerate. Then at mealtime, without taking the time to sauté, just add the nut-raisin-date mixture to the cracked wheat, heat and serve.

Bran Supplement: Add ¾ cup bran to cracked wheat if desired. But be sure to add ¼ cup water to cooking liquid if you supplement with bran.

Tabullah Salad—Traditional

SERVING TIME: 10 MINUTES
This is a salad, a main dish, and a wonderful high-fiber snack— good any time. The traditional recipe takes hardly any time, and you can do the "Super-Instant" version in about the time it takes to read this page.

1½ cups cracked wheat	*2–3 buds of garlic, minced*
4 large tomatoes, chopped	*1 8-ounce can tomato sauce*
5 or 6 scallions, chopped	*¼ cup olive oil*
¼ cup minced parsley	*Juice of 3 lemons*
2 large green peppers, chopped	*Salt and pepper to taste*

Soak cracked wheat in warm water for at least an hour. You can leave it soaking longer, and it won't be harmed. In the meantime chop the tomatoes, scallions, parsley, green peppers, and mince the garlic. Drain the cracked wheat and press out excess liquid. Toss with the vegetables, tomato sauce, olive oil, and lemon juice. Serves 6.

Quick and Easy (SERVING TIME: 5 MINUTES)
While you're doing something else, let the cracked wheat soak— the time isn't critical, just as long as it's at least an hour or so. The vegetables can also be prepared ahead of time. All you have to do is drain the cracked wheat and mix all the ingredients to- gether. That's it.

Super-Instant (SERVING TIME: 3 MINUTES)
About as instant as you can get. Use the following vegetables in dehydrated form:

2 tbsps. dehydrated onions	*2 tsps. parsley flakes*
2 tbsps. dehydrated green	*2 tsps. dehydrated chives*
peppers	*Juice of 3 lemons*
½-pound can of whole	
tomatoes with liquid	

Add the above to the presoaked cracked wheat, and you're all set.

Bran Supplement: ¾ cup bran if desired. But be sure to add ¼ cup more tomato sauce to the salad.

🪺🪺

If your family likes hot cereal—and especially if they *don't* like hot cereal—let them try the apple-honey-nut flavor of this recipe.

Cracked-Wheat Cereal—Traditional

SERVING TIME: 20 MINUTES

What makes this cereal different from the ordinary is the superb flavor of the cardamom-milk. You'll see when you taste it.

1 cup cracked wheat	*2 tbsps. nuts per serving*
2 cups water	*1 tbsp. honey per serving*
2 cups milk	*½ apple, chopped,* **or** *¼ cup*
1 tsp. ground cardamom seeds	*dried apples per serving*

In a 1½-quart saucepan put cracked wheat and water. Bring to a boil, lower heat and simmer, covered, 20 minutes. Makes about 3 cups. While the cracked wheat is cooking, heat the milk with the ground cardamom seeds; simmer. Serve the cracked wheat topped with the cardamom-milk, nuts, honey, and apples. Serves 4.

Variation:
Use dates, raisins, and chopped almonds.

Quick and Easy (SERVING TIME: 5 MINUTES)
Cook the cracked wheat the night before. Sometimes it's good to make double the recipe so that you can use part of it for other dishes including Anytime Wheat Cakes with Raisins and Nuts or Economy Cracked-Wheat Granola. When you're ready to serve this tasty cereal, simply heat it up, add warm milk with ground cardamom seeds, top with apples, nuts and honey and set it on the table.

Variation:
Soak 1 cup cracked wheat over night. In the morning drain and serve with the cardamom-milk, nuts, honey, and fruit.

Bran Supplement: Sprinkle 1 tablespoon bran over each serving if desired.

These are dollar-size delicacies that combine the best qualities of pancakes, fritters, and biscuits. They go well with fresh fruit, whipped cream, and a lot of other things.

Anytime Wheat Cakes with Raisins and Nuts— Traditional

SERVING TIME: 15 MINUTES

1 cup milk
2 eggs
2 tbsps. honey
1 tsp. vanilla
2 cups cooked cracked wheat (cooked as for preceding recipe) **or** *1 cup cracked*

wheat which has been soaked an hour or over night (and well drained)
¼ cup raisins
¼ cup chopped walnuts
¾ cup flour

In a blender mix milk, eggs, honey, and vanilla. Blend at high speed about 15 seconds. Add the cooked cracked wheat, raisins, and nuts. Mix by hand with a spoon. This mixture should be fairly thick. Grease and heat a griddle. Make silver-dollar-size cakes. Serve hot with honey and yogurt. Serves 4. Makes 24.

Quick and Easy (SERVING TIME: 8 MINUTES)
Prepare the batter mixture the night before. Store in refrigerator. Make griddle cakes fresh in the morning.

Super-Instant (SERVING TIME: 5 MINUTES)
Makes cakes ahead of time and freeze. Heat under broiler, carefully, turning once, or on greased griddle in seconds.

Bran Supplement: Add ½ cup bran and ¼ cup more milk.

🌀🌀

Make your own granola? Why not? It costs less, and you can vary the proportions to suit your own taste. After the first batch or two you will develop your own recipe—don't be afraid to improvise.

Super-Economy Cracked-Wheat Granola

SERVING TIME: 20 MINUTES

2 cups cracked wheat
2 cups rolled oats
1 cup sesame seeds
½ cup chopped pecans

½ chopped cashews
½ cup chopped walnuts
2 ounces ground cinnamon
½ tsp. cloves

Soak cracked wheat in water for at least an hour or over night. Drain and squeeze out excess moisture. Spread cracked wheat in thin layer on a cookie sheet and toast in preheated 400-degree oven for 20–30 minutes or until lightly browned. Mix several times while baking. On another cookie sheet, toast oats, seeds, and nuts for 7–8 minutes, stirring several times during baking. Cool and be sure the wheat is dry before combining with other ingredients. Add spices, mix well, and keep in airtight container. Serve with milk and honey or with yogurt, honey, and fresh fruit. Makes 6 cups.

Quick and Easy and Super-Instant
This recipe is best made up ahead of time, and so qualifies instantly as quick and easy and super-instant.

Bran Supplement: Sprinkle 1 tablespoon bran over cereal if desired.

Rice

First point—*wash the rice!* Many companies coat the grains with talc contaminated with asbestos. You don't need *that* on your menu. The basic concept of this rice dish and the others that follow is the porosity of rice grains. Each little sliver of rice soaks up the various flavors like a tiny thirsty sponge. Annatto seeds are no longer exotic; many supermarkets carry them in the spice section. They are excellent, but turmeric will do almost as well.

Mexican Rice—Traditional

SERVING TIME: 10 MINUTES

1 tbsp. annatto seeds. (If you are lucky enough to find those wonderful annatto seeds, sauté them in the butter for 3 minutes. Discard the seeds, add green pepper and garlic to the butter and continue as per instructions.) **or** *1 tbsp. turmeric*

2 cloves garlic, minced
1 small onion, chopped
1 small green pepper, chopped
3 tbsps. butter **or** *oil*
2 cups washed brown rice
3½ cups beef **or** *chicken stock*

In a heavy 2½–3-quart saucepan sauté the annatto seeds as stated above or turmeric with garlic, onion and green pepper in the butter for a minute or so at high heat. Add the rice and continue sautéeing until all the grains are coated and lightly browned, about 5 minutes. Add about one cup of the broth and stir constantly. The broth will be absorbed quickly. Add the rest of the broth and let boil, uncovered, for 20 minutes until most of the broth has been absorbed. Then cover, lower heat, and simmer about 20–30 minutes. This style of rice is distinctly different because it is tender, while being crunchy and flavorful. Serves 6.

Quick and Easy and Super-Instant (SERVING TIME: 5 MINUTES)
Cook up the rice ahead of time. Then all you have to do is heat, and you're ready to serve.

Bran Supplement: ¾ cup bran and ¼ cup more broth if desired.

🌀🌀

You have to watch the ingredients here. Obviously, the curry powder is the key. Imported India curry is the best—they've been in the business the longest. Watch out for gums and other additives in the cream, and don't use cloying sweetened coconut; if you can't find pure dried coconut, it's better to leave it out.

Curry Rice—Traditional

1 medium onion, chopped	*1½ tbsp. Madras curry powder*
1 tbsp. butter	*½ cup light cream*
2 cups washed brown rice	*½ cup raisins*
3½ cups beef **or** *chicken stock*	*½ cup dried coconut*

In a 2½–3-quart saucepan sauté the onion in the butter. Add rice and stir to cover each grain with the butter. Add stock and curry powder. Bring to a boil, lower heat, cover and simmer 30 minutes until the broth has been absorbed. Stir in light cream, raisins, coconut, and continue simmering, covered, about 10 minutes more. Serves 6.

You are welcome to write us about this recipe—or *any* recipe for that matter—but please don't say, "That's not the way *my* mother cooked Italian rice!" We know that. You are welcome to make it exactly the way she made it—just as long as you use brown rice. That's the one thing your mother probably *didn't* do. But your great-grandmother did it that way, and after you try it once, so will you.

Italian Rice—Traditional

2 cloves garlic, minced	*4 cups beef* **or** *chicken stock*
1 medium onion, chopped	*2 tsps. crushed oregano*
2 tbsps. olive oil	*½ cup Romano* **or** *Parmesan*
2 cups washed brown rice	*cheese*

In a 2½–3-quart saucepan sauté garlic and onion in the olive oil until onion becomes transparent. Add the rice, broth, and oregano and bring to a boil. Lower heat, cover and simmer 40 minutes. When rice is cooked and broth is absorbed, toss it with the cheese and serve. Serves 6.

Quick and Easy
Prepare the rice ahead of time. When you reheat it, before serving toss with the cheese.

Bran Supplement: Add ¾ cup bran to rice before cooking and ¼ cup more broth.

🍂 🍂

For all of us who have recoiled at the thought of struggling through a plate of pasty, starchy white rice, pilaf comes like a great bolt out of the blue. Recently, a flood of phony pilafs have been thrown on the market—tricked out in little plastic pokes and tabbed with cutesy names. They are basically awful white rice with a little packet of chemicals and spices inserted. Tastewise and nutritionwise—as they say on Madison Avenue—you'd probably do better to eat the plastic bag. Try real pilaf, and a whole new world will open up for you—don't be afraid as usual to add your own personal touch.

Basic Rice Pilaf—Traditional

SERVING TIME: 10 MINUTES

Cook 2 cups washed brown rice in:
2 tbsps. butter
4 tbsps. fine egg noodles, whole wheat
4 cups beef or chicken stock

Add to Cooked Rice:
2 tbsps. butter
1 onion, chopped
½ cup pignolia nuts or slivered almonds
¼ cup currants or raisins (½ cup, if you don't use dates)
¼ cup chopped dates (optional)
2 tsps. cinnamon
2 tsps. allspice

Melt the 2 tablespoons butter in a 2½–3-quart saucepan. Sauté egg noodles until light brown. Put in broth and rice and bring to a boil. When rice begins to boil, lower heat, cover, and simmer for 40–50 minutes. The rice is done when little holes appear on the surface of the pile of rice and the broth is absorbed.

While the rice is cooking, melt 2 tbsps. butter in a medium frying pan, and sauté onions until transparent. Add pignolia nuts, currants or raisins, dates if desired, cinnamon, and allspice. Mix well, sprinkle over rice and serve. Serves 6.

Quick and Easy (SERVING TIME: 5 MINUTES)
Cook the rice the night before. At dinnertime, sauté nut-raisin mixture with spices. Mix in with heated rice and serve.

Super-Instant (SERVING TIME: 3 MINUTES)
Cook the rice ahead of time. When heating the rice, add onion, raisins, nuts, and spices directly to the rice. Just heat and serve.

Bran Supplement: ¾ cup bran and ¼ cup more broth if desired.

Ah, what to do with leftover rice? These rice patties can even be eaten cold between meals—if they last that long.

Rice Patties—Traditional

SERVING TIME: 20 MINUTES

1 small onion, chopped
1 tbsp. olive oil
1½ cups beef **or** *chicken stock*
¾ cup washed brown rice
¾ cup Parmesan cheese
¾ cup crushed bran flakes

1 tsp. freshly ground black pepper
2 tsps. crushed sage leaves
2 eggs
Olive oil; begin with ¼ cup, and add a little more if needed

In a 1-quart saucepan sauté onion in oil a minute or so. Add liquid and rice. Bring to a boil. When rice begins to boil, lower heat, cover, and simmer for 45 minutes. Toss the Parmesan cheese with the rice. Mix the bran with the black pepper and sage. Beat the eggs well and add to rice. Make round or oval shaped patties with the rice-cheese mixture. Dip the patties into the bran-spice mixture, coating each side well. Put ¼ cup of olive oil in the frying pan and heat to a medium-high heat. Fry the patties until browned on both sides, drain on layers of paper towels, and serve. Makes 24 cakes. Or, place on greased cookie sheet and bake at preheated 400-degrees for 15–20 minutes. Serves 6 to 8.

Quick and Easy
Use already-cooked brown rice, prepare the patties, fry and serve, or bake as directed above.

Super-Instant
These patties can be made ahead of time and just reheated in the oven at dinnertime. They can be frozen, ready for any meal-time.

Bran Supplement: Already included in this recipe.

Oats

For most people, hot oatmeal cereal brings up all kinds of associations: Oliver Twist's plate of gruel, lumps floating in clumps, and ready-mix cement. We offer this recipe as compensation for all past suffering.

Oatmeal Cereal—Traditional

SERVING TIME: 15 MINUTES

1 cup rolled oats
3 cups milk
1 tbsp. cinnamon
2 tsps. almond flavoring
1 tbsp. raisins per serving

1 tbsp. chopped almonds per serving
1 tbsp. sesame seeds per serving

In a 1½-quart saucepan put oats and milk. Bring to a boil, then simmer about 15 minutes. Add the cinnamon and almond flavoring. Serve with more milk, raisins, almonds, and sesame seeds. Serves 4.

Quick and Easy (SERVING TIME: 5 MINUTES)
Cook the oatmeal the night before with the cinnamon and almond flavoring. In the morning just heat and serve with milk, raisins, almonds, and sesame seeds.

Check the label on the commercial TV-advertised versions of this excellent menu item. Choke back your indignation, and then sit down and enjoy these tasty little high-fiber squares.

High-Fiber Breakfast Cakes—Traditional

SERVING TIME: 15 MINUTES

1½ cups whole-wheat pastry
  flour
1½ cups rolled oats
½ tsp. baking soda
½ cup butter
½ cup honey
1½ cups chopped dates
  (10 ounces pitted)

2 tbsps. honey
1 cup water
1 cup chopped nuts
⅛ tsp. cloves
1 tsp. cinnamon
½ tsp. ginger

Mix flour, oats, and baking soda. Cut in butter, and blend until crumbly. Stir in ½ cup honey. Spread half the mixture in a thin layer in bottom of a greased 8 x 8 pan. In a saucepan bring to a boil dates, honey, and water. Boil, stirring constantly, about 5 minutes. Remove from heat, and add nuts and spices. Spread the date mixture over oat mixture in pan. Spread remaining oat-flour mixture over the date-nut mixture. Bake in preheated oven for 40 minutes. Serves 8.

Variation:
Chop 6 apples and mix with ½ cup water and ¼ cup honey. Bring to a boil and let boil, stirring constantly for 5 minutes. Remove from heat and stir in nuts, 1 tablespoon cinnamon, and ½ teaspoon ginger. Use in place of date-nut mixture.

Buckwheat

Buckwheat originated in India centuries ago. The French gave it the romantic name of Blé Sarrasin, or "Wheat of the Saracens." This noble and fiber-filled grain deserves a better fate than a minor role in somebody's "Genuine Buckwheat [flavored] Pancake Mix with imitation butter nuggets . . ." Try buckwheat cakes and you'll know why the world feared the Saracens.

Buckwheat Cakes—Traditional

SERVING TIME: 25 MINUTES

1½ cups beef or chicken stock
½ cup buckwheat
½ cup cream cheese or ricotta
¼ cup chopped fresh dill or 2
 tsps. dry dill weed
2 eggs, beaten

¾ cup bran (approx.)
½ tsp. freshly ground black
 pepper
Small amount of oil or butter
Sour cream
More fresh dill to top cakes

In a 1-quart saucepan bring the broth to a boil. Add buckwheat, stir and cook for a minute at high heat, then lower heat, then cover and simmer for 8–10 minutes until broth is absorbed. Cool, then mix the cooked buckwheat with cream cheese or ricotta, dill, and beaten eggs. Shape into cakes, dip into the bran mixed with black pepper. Fry in a small amount of oil or butter, preferably in a black cast-iron pan, until golden brown. Serve these with sour cream and more chopped dill on top. Makes 6 cakes.

Quick and Easy (SERVING TIME: 15 MINUTES)
Prepare the buckwheat ahead of time. Before dinner assemble the ingredients, shape and fry the cakes and serve.

Super-Instant
Make the cakes ahead and freeze. Warm these on a hot greased griddle or in a preheated oven at 400 degrees about 15 minutes. Top with sour cream and dried dill.

Bran Supplement: Already included above.

🐦🦜

Buckwheat is probably the least appreciated of all grains. It is full-bodied, chewy, and contains twenty-five times the fiber of white rice—as well as about twice the protein. But don't take our word for it; try it and you'll see what we mean.

Buckwheat Casserole—Traditional

2¼ cups chicken stock	4 tbsps. whole-wheat flour
¾ cup buckwheat, whole or split	4 cups milk
1 tbsp. butter	½ tsp. freshly ground black pepper
1 medium onion, chopped	2 cups shredded cheddar cheese
3 tbsps. butter	

Preheat oven to 375 degrees. In a 1½–2-quart saucepan put chicken stock and buckwheat. Bring to a boil and then cover and simmer for about 7 minutes, until the broth is absorbed. In a casserole, about a 3-quart size, sauté the onion in the one tablespoon of butter. In a saucepan melt the rest of the butter. Blend in the flour until it becomes a paste. Add the milk gradually, stirring constantly, until the mixture thickens. Add the black pepper and 1½ cups of the cheese. Stir until the cheese melts. Mix the cooked buckwheat with the onion in the casserole. Pour the milk-cheese mixture over the buckwheat. Sprinkle the top with the remaining cheese and bake until the top browns a bit, about 30 minutes. Serves 6.

Cornmeal

These are so good there is nothing we can say about them—
they speak for themselves.

Corn Cakes—Traditional

1 cup hot milk
1 cup stone-ground white
    cornmeal

2 eggs
2 tbsps. honey

Blend hot milk and cornmeal in a blender at low speed for a
minute or so. While the blender is blending carefully add the eggs
one at a time. Add the honey. Blend for a few seconds longer.
This mixture will be thin. It makes very tender corn cakes. Stir
batter frequently. Grease a hot griddle, drop the batter by tablespoons, making silver-dollar-size corn cakes. Top with honey or
molasses. Makes about 30 cakes.

Quick and Easy
Make the mixture the night before and cook it in the morning.

Super-Instant
Make the cakes ahead of time and stack with pieces of waxed
paper in between. Store in refrigerator if you're going to use them
within the next day or two or freeze them. To serve, warm the
cakes in the oven on a greased cookie sheet at 375 degrees or
carefully under the broiler (at the second level from the top), or
warm them in seconds on a greased griddle.

Bran Supplement: ½ cup bran and ¼ cup more milk.

🐚🐚

These are really a cross between mini-corn dumplings, Chinese
eggdrops, and spatzle—with more fiber and richer flavor (we

think) than any of them. Keep an open mind, and you'll find more ways to use them than you ever imagined.

Corn-Drop Noodles—Traditional

SERVING TIME: 20 MINUTES

2 quarts beef **or** *chicken stock*
Put this on the stove to come to a boil in a large frying pan while you are making the noodle dough.

2 cups cornmeal	*1 cup whole-wheat pastry flour*
2 cups boiling water	*2 eggs, beaten*

Mix the cornmeal with the boiling water, stirring well. When the mixture cools, add flour and eggs. The batter should be very thick. Drop the noodle dough by small spoonfuls into the boiling stock, cooking them about 2–3 minutes. Only cook a layer of noodles at a time. Remove with a slotted spoon to a bowl and toss with a small amount of butter. Serve this at the side of sauced chicken or with a beef stew. Corn noodles can also be served with a spicy tomato sauce or, for those who love garlic, tossed with the butter and fresh minced garlic. Serves 6.

Wheat Berry

Nothing compares with the "wheaty" flavor of the intact wheat berry. It's great as a poultry stuffing, but it can stand on its own very nicely.

Wheat Berry Stove-Top Stuffing—Traditional

SERVING TIME: 10 MINUTES

2 tbsps. butter	*1½ tsps. crushed or ground*
3 cloves garlic, minced	*cumin*
2 medium onions, chopped	*2 tsps. crushed dried oregano*
1 green pepper, chopped	*1 bay leaf*
1 large tomato, chopped	*1 cup whole wheat berries*
2 cups beef **or** *chicken stock*	*Juice of 1 lemon*

In a 2-quart saucepan sauté garlic, onions, and green pepper for about 2 minutes. Add tomato and sauté another minute. Add broth, cumin, oregano, bay leaf, and whole wheat berries. Bring to a boil, lower heat, cover and simmer for 40 minutes. When cooked add lemon juice. Use as stuffing for roasting chicken or beef roll. Makes 6 cups stuffing.

This is deliciously chewy and can be eaten just as a side dish if you wish, but it adds a lot of flavoring as a stuffing.

Quick and Easy (SERVING TIME: 5 MINUTES)
Prepare this ahead of time and stuff it cold into the chicken or beef roll. Or serve it heated as a side dish.

Super-Instant (SERVING TIME: 5 MINUTES)
If you're in a hurry when you prepare this ahead of time then use the following ingredients:

2 tbsps. dehydrated onions	*1 cup broth*
1 tbsp. dehydrated green pepper	*1 tsp. powdered garlic*
per	*1 can whole wheat berries*
1 8-ounce can of tomato sauce	

In the butter sauté the dehydrated onions and peppers for a minute or so. Add tomato sauce, broth, garlic, and whole wheat berries and proceed as above, allowing the whole wheat to cook for 40 minutes.

Bran Supplement: ½ cup bran added to whole wheat before it is cooked.

Barley

Barley is the neglected grain. It has more than half the protein of sirloin steak, a good bit of fiber, and a fresh new taste. (Get the "Scotch" or "Pot" variety.)

Barley Casserole—Traditional

SERVING TIME: 15 MINUTES

2 tbsps. butter **or** oil
3–4 cloves garlic, minced
2 medium onions, chopped
¼ cup fresh chopped dill
½ pound fresh mushrooms,
    sliced

1½ cups barley
3 cups chicken stock
Juice of 1 lemon
½ tsp. freshly ground black
    pepper

In a 3-quart saucepan over high heat, sauté garlic, onions, dill, and mushrooms in the oil or butter until the liquid from the mushrooms evaporates, stirring constantly.

Add barley, chicken stock, lemon juice, and black pepper; mix well. Bring to a boil, then lower heat and simmer, covered, for 25 minutes. Serves 6.

Quick and Easy (SERVING TIME: 15 MINUTES)
Prepare the barley the day before. Sauté onions, mushrooms, and spices. Mix with barley and ¼ cup more broth. Heat and serve.

Super-Instant (SERVING TIME: 5 MINUTES)
To the already cooked barley add 1 tablespoon dried dill, 2 tablespoons dehydrated onions, 2 8-ounce cans of mushrooms, and ¼ cup broth. Heat and serve.

Bran Supplement: Add ¾ cup bran and 1 cup more broth.

Barley Instant Breakfast has everything going for it: low cost, new flavor, high fiber, and the convenience of a one-dish breakfast. Good-bye, Toast-Em Pop-Ups!

Barley Instant Breakfast

SERVING TIME: 10 MINUTES

This wonderful dish is easy to prepare ahead of time and makes a sensational high-fiber breakfast. It doesn't have to be reheated, and the kids can help themselves.

1 cup barley	*2 cups chopped walnuts*
1½ quarts water	*2 tbsps. rosewater*
1 cup raisins	*2 tsps. vanilla*
1 cup chopped dried apricots	*Juice of half a lemon*
½ cup honey	

Place barley and water in a 2½–3-quart pot and bring to a boil. Lower heat and simmer 1½ hours. Add raisins, apricots, and honey, and simmer another 30 minutes. Put this into a deep bowl. Add nuts, rosewater, vanilla, and juice of half a lemon, and cool. Rosewater is the secret ingredient and makes this a fragrant delicious instant breakfast. (Rosewater can be purchased at most pharmacies.) Serves 6.

This can be cooking in the evening while you're watching TV or just relaxing. It doesn't require much attention, but your family will give it a lot of attention at breakfast.

For even more convenience, Barley Instant Breakfast can be made firmer and higher in protein in the following way:

In ¼ cup of cold water, moisten 2 packets of unflavored gelatin. Add to the barley pot at the end of the cooking time. Stir well to be sure that the gelatin dissolves. Then remove pot from stove and add nuts, rosewater, vanilla, and juice of half a lemon. Pour into greased loaf pans and chill. Unmold and slice. The cooked barley retains flavors of the liquid it was cooked in. Actually, you might prefer the dill-flavored barley for breakfast and the water-cooked barley with honey and lemon for dessert. But either way, you can't go wrong.

Barley Cakes—Traditional

1 cup milk   ¾ cup whole-wheat flour
2 eggs   2 cups cooked barley
2 tbsps. honey

In a blender put milk, eggs, and honey, and blend at high speed for a minute or so. Add flour and blend again at high speed for a few seconds until the flour is well blended. Add the barley, and with a spoon mix the barley into the mixture. Bake the cakes on a hot, well-greased griddle, dropping the batter in tablespoonfuls. Makes about 18 cakes.

If the barley was cooked in water, serve the cakes for breakfast with honey and lemon if desired. If the barley was made with broth, add dill or mint to the batter and serve as a side dish with the evening meal.

Quick and Easy
Make the batter up the day before and have it ready for when you need it.

Super-Instant
Make these cakes as much as one week in advance and freeze. Warm them at the second level from the top under the broiler, turn them once and watch them carefully, or warm them on a greased griddle in seconds.

Bran Supplement: ½ cup bran and ¼ cup more milk.

Don't take our word for it, but barley and chicken seem to be made for each other.

Barley Stuffing for Chicken—Traditional

SERVING TIME: 10 MINUTES

(4–5 pound roasting chicken)
1 tbsp. butter
4 cloves garlic, minced
1 small onion, chopped fine
1 medium green pepper,
chopped fine
¼ cup chopped celery

3 tbsps. freshly chopped mint
¼ tsp. freshly ground black
pepper
1 cup barley
2 cups chicken stock
Juice of half a lemon

In a 1½–2-quart saucepan sauté minced garlic in butter until the garlic is lightly browned. Add onion, green pepper, celery, mint, and black pepper. Sauté quickly about one minute. Add barley and mix well to coat each grain with the butter. Add chicken stock and lemon juice, and bring to a boil. Lower heat, cover, and simmer for 25 minutes. Set aside to cool. The barley will not be completely cooked, and there will still be some liquid. (See p. 96 for chicken recipe.)

Quick and Easy (SERVING TIME: 15 MINUTES)

1 tsp. powdered garlic
1 tbsp. dehydrated onions
1 tbsp. dehydrated green
peppers

½ tsp. celery seeds
1 tbsp. dried mint
¼ tsp. ground black pepper
1 tbsp. lemon juice

In a 1½–2-quart saucepan put butter, above dried spices, barley, stock, and lemon juice. Proceed as in above recipe.

Super-Instant
Cook barley the day before, using only barley and stock, or use 3–4 cups of already cooked barley. Add dried spices and ¼ cup more broth. Mix and stuff chicken.

Bran Supplement: ½ cup bran may be added to the barley stuffing, plus ¼ cup more broth.

5

Bread & Pastries

Remember when bread used to be called "The Staff of Life"? Now it's more like a rod to punish the poor consumer. The contents of the average loaf of commercial white "bread" tell the story eloquently. That's the kind of bread the manufacturers refer to among themselves as "balloon bread," because it's whipped up with air to make it look bigger than it really is. The only one that gets whipped is the one who buys it. And just to give the customer an extra zing, the standard loaf is often 15 ounces—not the pound of bread that everyone unconsciously expects. Steal an ounce from a hundred million loaves of bread and you get about six million extra loaves free. That adds up to two and a half million dollars at retail every day. But that kind of cheating is small time compared to nutritional swindle that goes on. Let's compare a pound of commercial white bread with a pound of commercial whole wheat. (Source: U.S.D.A. Handbook No. 8. Values are for one pound, since the reference book was written before the "15 ounce pound" became standard.)

WHOLE-WHEAT BREAD (WITH 2 PERCENT NONFAT DRY MILK)	ENRICHED WHITE BREAD (WITH 2 PERCENT NONFAT DRY MILK)
1102 calories (11 percent fewer calories)	1220 calories
47.6 grams of protein	39.5 grams of protein
216 grams of carbohydrates	228 grams of carbohydrates
13 milligrams of niacin	318 milligrams of calcium
449 milligrams of calcium	10 milligrams of niacin
1000 milligrams of phosphorous	395 milligrams of phosphorous

Whole-wheat bread has 20 percent more protein, 6 percent less fat, 5 percent less carbohydrate, 41 percent more calcium, 160 percent more phosphorus, 220 percent more potassium, 24 percent more niacin, about the same amount of thiamine and slightly *less* riboflavin than *enriched* white bread. But that's only the beginning of the story. *Whole-wheat bread contains 800 percent more fiber than white bread!* And much more *usable* vitamins and minerals than even the official U.S. government figures indicate.

Even more interesting is the deception of "enriching" flour. The way the bakers brag on the labels: "Made from ENRICHED white flour according to U.S. Government Standards!" you would think those pathetic bloated lumps of balloon bread were a useful addition to your diet. The real facts are fascinating. Back in 1952 the federal officials who guide our destinies noticed that Americans were eating a lot of bread. They also detected the fact that the white "bread" which was being consumed wasn't bread at all—in the technical sense. So they commanded the corporate bakers to "enrich" the "product," as they call it, by adding the following minimum amounts of vitamins and iron per pound: Thiamine: 1.1 mg.; riboflavin: .7 mg.; niacin: 10 mg.; iron: 8 mg.; and calcium: 0 mg.

Just to put it in perspective, a milligram is one thousandth of a gram, and there are about 460 grams in a pound; the cost of "enrichment" is hardly a burden to the baking industry. That gaily printed plastic wrapper costs far more than all the vitamins and iron added to the balloon loaf. To complete the panorama, the vitamins are of course synthetic vitamins which are probably not absorbed completely, and the iron is generally inorganic iron—similar to the rust on nails—which is difficult or impossible for many people to assimilate. In contrast, the vitamins and minerals in whole-wheat bread are in their natural organic state ready to enter the human body in abundance.

Those are the scientific reasons not to eat commercial "white bread." Certainly they apply equally well to all the other "breads" that clutter the "bread" section of the supermarket: raisin-nut bread, "French" bread, "Italian" bread, and all the permutations of balloon bread made with "enriched" white flour. But there is an equally compelling reason to shun those pseudo-breads: the bakers have dumped a chemistry set into your "staff of life." Here are some of the things they put into the bread that you feed your kids to help them "build up their bodies": diacetyl tartaric acid, calcium carbonate, calcium sulfate, potassium iodate, sodium propionate, lactylic stearate, succinnylated monoglycerides, ethoxylated diglycerides, and sodium stearyl fumarate.

Remember too that the bakeries hire processors—none of whom look healthy themselves—to insist that none of those chemicals are harmful. The fact that these "consultants" are paid up to $1000 a day to tell you how yummy these chemicals are should also be taken into consideration in making up your mind. I think one charming lady summed it up when she wrote to me on that subject:

"Dr. Reuben,

If I ever get a taste for lactylic stearate or ethoxylated diglycerides, why, I'll just go out to the store and buy some! Until then, I'm going to bake my own bread."

Beyond all nutritional and health considerations, there is one overriding reason to make your own breads and pastries: they taste better! You are blending the finest of ingredients in the most devoted way to please and nourish your family. No mushy mess churned out by indifferent machines can come close to your results. One final word. There has been a constant and intensifying campaign in television advertising to convince the women of America that they should leave the food preparation to gigantic corporations. You've seen it: "Leave the fuss to us!" and "Making it from scratch is old-fashioned, Mother!" and "Save yourself the trouble of suffering in the kitchen!" Perhaps it's more important to save all that suffering in the cancer ward or the cardiac-care unit. Put the fiber back into your bread and baked goods, get the chemicals out, and begin to enjoy eating and cooking again. Once you go through the first few recipes you'll see how quick and easy—and satisfying—it is to do. Start off with the Raisin Quick Bread on page 56, then try the bread sticks on page 55. By the time you've done these, you'll have kicked the balloon bread habit for life.

Bread

Making bread and pastries is the easiest thing in the world. If you can drive a car, zip up your dress from behind, or (in the case of male cooks) assemble your kid's new tricycle at Christmas, then you can make perfect bread and pastries. There are a few things that will help you from the outset. First, get a good blender. Look underneath the unit for the wattage of the motor, which is a rough indication of its power: 800 watts and up is the right idea. Push buttons don't mean anything—two speeds, fast and slow, are just fine.

A good mixer will help a lot—again, a powerful motor is essential. A model with a "dough hook" will make kneading bread a cinch, but remember this is a situation where brute horse-power and quality engineering will pay off. A pastry blender also comes in handy—it's just a series of knife-blades on a handle to mix dough and shortening quickly.

Of course, you can bake superb bread and pastries without any equipment except a table, a bowl, a mixing spoon, and an oven, but you might as well make things easy for yourself—the whole philosophy of The Save-Your-Life Diet is to make life longer and more enjoyable—and that applies to cooking as well.

Recipes

This is one of those wonderful "nothing can go wrong" recipes. Just mix the dough to the consistency of, say, thick silly putty, form the sticks, and you're in business. Which proves once and for all that making bread at home is easy. This procedure takes about 5 minutes longer than (ugh!) "brown-and-serve," and will make you feel better seven ways.

Baton Salé—Traditional

SERVING TIME: 20 MINUTES

2–3 cups stone-ground whole-
wheat flour
1 cup bran
1 cup butter, melted
1 egg

Sesame seeds (Start with ½ cup
and then add what you need.)
½ cup water
1 tsp. baking powder
Egg yolks for glaze (Start with
one yolk.)

On a bread board or counter put 2 cups of flour and the bran, and make a well in the middle. In the well pour the butter and begin to mix in the flour. Add the egg, water, baking powder, and gradually mix in as much flour as is necessary to make a nice soft dough, smooth, unsticky, and elastic. Make bread sticks. Brush the sticks with beaten egg yolks, roll the sticks in sesame seeds and place them on greased cookie sheets. Bake in a pre-heated 350-degree oven for 20–30 minutes. Makes 3–4 dozen sticks.

🐟🐟

This is the next step after making the baton salé. Kneading the dough for 15–20 minutes is physical and emotional therapy— try it and you'll see. However, if you have a *good* mixer with a dough hook, you can do yoga instead; kneading time is 5–7 minutes.

Bread Sticks—Traditional

SERVING TIME: 20–35 MINUTES

4 cups stone-ground whole-wheat flour (approx.)
1 cup bran
1 cup melted butter
2 eggs
2 packages yeast or 2 tbsps. yeast dissolved in ⅓ cup warm water with a touch of honey added. Let stand a few minutes. It will rise.

1 tsp. baking powder
¼ cup black caraway seeds (can be found in most Greek or Middle Eastern markets and makes these sticks very special) or 1 cup sunflower seeds
1 cup milk (approx.)

On a large bread board or counter put the flour and the bran, and make a well in the mound of flour and bran. In the well pour the butter, and begin to mix in the flour a bit at a time. Then add the eggs and yeast mixture, and work more of the flour into it. Then add the baking powder, caraway seeds, and milk, a little at a time, constantly working in more and more of the flour, using only what you need to make a nice soft dough. Knead the dough well—about 15–20 minutes, until it is smooth and elastic. Grease cookie sheets. Pinch off small pieces of dough and roll into bread sticks. Brush the tops with beaten egg. Bake the sticks in a preheated 350-degree oven for about 15 minutes. Makes 5–6 dozen sticks.

Bran Supplement: Already included.

🐝🦋

When we say "quick bread," we mean quick! Gather the ingredients, pop into the mixing bowl, snap on the mixer, toss in the nuts, whirl again—and into the pan and the oven. Sixty minutes later, you get your reward.

Whole-Wheat Raisin and Nut Quick Bread—Traditional

SERVING TIME: 5 MINUTES

3 cups whole-wheat flour
3 tsps. baking powder
1 cup honey, or ½ honey and
    ½ molasses
1¼ cups milk
1 cup raisins

1 cup chopped nuts—walnuts
    or pecans
2 tbsps. melted butter
1 tbsp. cinnamon
¼ tsp. nutmeg

Preheat oven to 325 degrees. Grease a bread loaf pan, 9x5x3, and line bottom with waxed paper. In a mixing bowl beat together well all the ingredients except the raisins and nuts. Add the raisins and nuts and mix again. Pour the quick bread into the prepared pan. Bake for one hour. Turn onto a rack to cool.

Bran Supplement: Add 1 cup bran and ¼ cup more milk.

This is a rich, sweet bread, almost in the pastry class—but no refined sugar, no junky ingredients, and plenty of protein from the milk, nuts, and eggs. Try it with homemade ice cream for a dessert you'll never forget.

Apple-Nut Quick Bread—Traditional

SERVING TIME: 5–7 MINUTES

3 cups whole-wheat flour
3 tsps. baking powder
2 tbsps. cinnamon
1 tsp. ginger
1 tsp. allspice
1 cup honey

1 cup milk
2 eggs
4 tbsps. melted butter
1 cup chopped nuts
2 cups chopped fresh apples

Preheat oven to 325 degrees. Grease a loaf pan, 9x5x3, and line bottom with waxed paper. In a mixing bowl put flour, baking powder, cinnamon, ginger, and allspice. Add honey, milk, and eggs, and blend well. Then add the melted butter, and beat again. Add the nuts and apples, and mix well. Pour the mixture into prepared pan and bake 50 minutes to an hour.

Bran Supplement: Add 1 cup bran and ¼ cup milk.

🌀🌀

Steaming gives a special flavor to bread, and the steamer doesn't have to be anything fancy. Just take a big soup pot with a cover, set a wide can—like a fish can—with both ends cut off, on the bottom (to keep the dough pan out of the water) and fill the pot with a few inches of water. Set the heat just high enough to make a small head of steam, cover, and in 20 minutes you will have a plateful of rolls that no money can buy.

Steamed Yeast Rolls—Traditional

SERVING TIME: 12–20 MINUTES

1 package yeast or 1 tbsp. yeast, dissolved in ¼ cup warm water with 2 tsps. honey	*4 cups stone-ground whole-wheat flour*
	2 tbsps. melted butter
	1½–2 cups water (approx.)

In a cup mix yeast, water, and honey, and let stand a few minutes. Place the flour on a board, make a well in the middle, and pour in the butter. Gradually work in the flour, then add the yeast mixture and as much of the water as is needed to make a soft dough. Place the dough in a greased bowl, cover with a damp towel and place in a warm place. Let rise until double in bulk (about 2 hours). Punch down and divide the dough into about 24 pieces. Shape each into a round or rectangular roll. Place on a wide plate that will fit into steamer. Cover and let rise again until doubled (about 1 hour). Place in steamer and steam for 20 minutes.

Bran Supplement: Add 1 cup bran and ¼ cup more water.

🐚🐚

All of you who have been slaves to packaged biscuit mixes, arise and throw off your chains! This recipe will save you at least 50 percent in cost and add about 550 percent in flavor (conservative estimate). If you can't kick the biscuit-mix habit, you can put the bran, whole-wheat flour, and baking powder into a tightly closed jar ahead of time. As far as greasing the baking sheet is concerned, don't use an aerosol spray—unless you want a non-stick coating on your lungs. Use butter, oil—almost anything else.

Biscuits—Traditional

SERVING TIME: 10 MINUTES

2 cups stone-ground whole-wheat flour	3 tsps. baking powder
	⅓ cup cold butter
1 cup bran	¾–1 cup milk

Preheat oven to 450 degrees. Combine the dry ingredients in a mixing bowl. Cut the butter into pieces into the bowl. With a pastry blender or two knives, cut the butter into the flour until the mixture is crumbly. Gradually add the milk until you have a soft dough. Turn the dough out onto a lightly floured board, and knead gently with floured fingers for a few turns. Roll out about ½ inch thick. Cut biscuits 2½–3 inches in diameter. Place the biscuits on a greased baking sheet, and bake for about 12–15 minutes. Makes 12 biscuits.

Variations:
• For drop biscuits, increase the milk to 1¼ cups. The dough should be moist enough to drop the biscuits from a spoon.

· Cheese: Add ½ cup grated cheddar to drop biscuits. Add ¼ cup Parmesan cheese to "cut" biscuits.

Bran Supplement: Already included.

🦋 🦋

We recommend cast-iron muffin tins for these; they add iron to the diet—at no cost—cook magnificiently, and look great hanging on the kitchen wall. Note to emancipated wives: You won't have any trouble getting your husband to whip these up, and it's a good way to show him cooking can be fun. Preparation time is about the length of two white "bread" TV commercials.

Whole-Wheat Muffins—Traditional

SERVING TIME: 5 MINUTES

2 cups stone-ground whole-wheat flour	*3 eggs*
2 tsps. baking powder	*1¼ cups milk*
	4 tbsps. melted butter

Preheat oven to 425 degrees. Put all ingredients in mixing bowl and mix only enough to blend. Pour into greased muffin tins about two-thirds full. Bake for 20–25 minutes.

Variations (Add to whole-wheat muffin recipe):
· Cheese: Add 1 cup grated cheddar or ½ cup Parmesan.
· Dried Fruit: Add ½ cup raisins, chopped apricots, chopped dates, or chopped figs.
· Fresh Fruit: Add 1 cup blueberries, chopped fresh pineapple, chopped apples, or mashed bananas, plus ¼ cup honey.
· Nuts: Add 1 cup chopped nuts of your choice.
· Oatmeal: Add 1 cup rolled oats and increase milk to 1½ cups.
· Yogurt or Buttermilk: Substitute for milk and add ½ teaspoon baking soda.

Bran Supplement: Add 1 cup bran and ¼ cup more milk.

Did you really think that the elegant English ever served soggy little half-cooked muffins with their superb British breakfasts? Of course not! Those miserable little atrocities that come in plastic sacks are barred from British soil. These are English muffins worthy of the name, and when you turn out your first batch, you'll see what we mean.

High-Fiber English Muffins—Traditional

SERVING TIME: 12–20 MINUTES

3 cups stone-ground whole-wheat flour (approx.)
1¼ cups water
1 tbsp. honey
1 cup bran

1 package yeast or 1 tbsp. yeast, dissolved in ¼ cup warm water with a touch of honey. Let stand for a few minutes and watch it rise.
1 egg

In a bowl put half the flour, and the water, honey, bran, yeast which has risen, and egg. Mix well. Then add as much of the rest of the flour as needed to make a soft dough, turning out the dough onto a bread board or counter so that you can knead it well . . . 15 minutes or so, until dough is smooth. Place the dough in a greased bowl, cover with a towel and place in a warm place to rise double in size—about 2 hours. Punch down, and turn the dough onto a lightly floured board or counter. Roll out the dough ½ inch thick and cut rounds 2½ to 3 inches in diameter with a floured cookie cutter or the rim of a glass. Place the rounds on a greased, cornmealed cookie sheet. Cover with a damp cloth and let rise about an hour. Remove cloth. Cover the tops of the muffins with an ungreased cookie sheet, using it as a weight, and place the muffins in a preheated 375-degree oven about 20–25 minutes, or until the muffins are lightly browned. Cool muffins on a rack. Makes a dozen 3-inch muffins.

Bran Supplement: Already included.

🐚🐚

Grandmother came from Scotland, and these are her scones—the only thing we added was the pecans, which don't grow well in Scotland. You'll be happy with these.

Grandmother's Oatmeal Scones—Traditional

SERVING TIME: 15 MINUTES

1 cup oats
1¾ cups stone-ground whole-wheat flour
1 tsp. baking soda
½ cup cold butter (1 stick)

½ cup chopped pecans
¾–1 cup milk
1 tbsp. vinegar
2 tbsps. honey

Mix the dry ingredients. Cut in the butter until the mixture is crumbly. Stir in pecans. Add milk mixed with vinegar and honey, and toss lightly. Make little cakes—which are rolled or just patted —about ¼ inch thick. Bake on a hot greased griddle over low heat for 10 minutes, or until well risen. Increase heat to medium and brown underside for about 6 minutes. Turn and brown other side (about 5 minutes). Serve with homemade preserves or honey. Makes 8 scones about 2½ inches in diameter. Serves 4.

Quick and Easy (SERVING TIME: 7 MINUTES)
Make up the dough the night before. Bake the scones fresh in the morning.

Super-Instant (SERVING TIME: 4 MINUTES)
This is another recipe which can be made up ahead of time and frozen. These may be warmed in the toaster or on the griddle in seconds.

Bran Supplement: ½ cup bran and just enough more milk to make a nice dough.

If you've been a slave to the franchise doughnut shop down in the shopping center, this can be your year of independence. You can also upgrade your intake of fiber, reduce your dose of chemicals, and discover what a *real* doughnut tastes like.

Raised Whole-Wheat Doughnuts—Traditional

SERVING TIME: 12–20 MINUTES

1 cup milk
½ cup butter
1 cup honey
1 package yeast or 1 tbsp. yeast, dissolved in ¼ cup warm water with a touch of honey

3 eggs
1 cup bran
4½–5½ cups stone-ground whole-wheat flour
1 tsp. mace

Scald the milk, take it off the heat, and put in butter and honey to dissolve together in the hot milk. Let cool. In a cup dissolve the yeast as directed, and let stand a few minutes. It will rise. In a mixing bowl beat eggs. Add the milk-butter-honey mixture and beat in the bran with a couple of cups of the flour and the mace. Add the yeast mixture and more flour until the mixer begins to labor. Then turn the dough out onto a floured board and begin to knead in the rest of the flour—enough to make a soft dough. If your mixer has a dough hook, use it to do the kneading. Knead well. Turn dough into a greased bowl and let rise in a warm place until doubled in bulk (about 2 hours). Turn the dough onto a lightly floured board and roll out about ½ inch in thickness. Cut out doughnuts with doughnut cutter or a wide-mouthed jar. Place the rounds on a greased cookie sheet and let rise about an hour. Fry the doughnuts in deep oil heated to about 370 degrees, turning them when they begin to rise. Use a candy thermometer to watch temperature—do not let it get above 375 degrees. Turn them a couple of times until lightly browned.

Drain on several layers of paper toweling. Makes 3 dozen doughnuts.

❦ ❧

The basic difference between cake doughnuts and raised doughnuts is the yeast in the raised variety—plus the extra waiting time for the dough to rise. Either way, they're good!

Whole-Wheat Cake Doughnuts—Traditional

SERVING TIME: 20–30 MINUTES

2 eggs
1 cup honey
3 tbsps. melted butter
1 cup bran
4–4½ cups stone-ground whole-wheat flour

5 tsps. baking powder
1 tbsp. cinnamon
¼ tsp. nutmeg
¼ tsp. mace
¾ cup milk

Break the eggs into a mixing bowl and beat until light. Add the honey and continue beating. Blend in the butter. Add dry ingredients alternately with the milk. On a lightly floured board, turn out the dough and roll it about ½ inch thick. Cut with floured doughnut cutter and fry in deep oil, heated to about 370 degrees, until they rise to surface and are brown on one side. Then turn and brown other side. Drain on several thicknesses of paper toweling. Use a candy thermometer to keep the temperature around 370 degrees, not higher than 375 degrees. This bit of care will help make superb doughnuts. Makes 38–40 donuts.

Bran Supplement: Already included.

❦ ❧

These are 100 percent buckwheat pancakes—not pasty white flour dusted with a bit of buckwheat. Words cannot describe them—just make them up and you'll never regret it.

Buckwheat Pancakes—Traditional

SERVING TIME: 15 MINUTES

2 cups milk
1 tbsp. butter **or** oil
¼ cup warm water
½ package, or 1½ tsps. yeast

2 tbsps. molasses
2 cups buckwheat flour
1 egg, slightly beaten

The night before scald the milk, add the butter or oil and set aside to cool. Put the warm water into a large bowl with the yeast and molasses. Mix well. Let stand a minute or so to let it rise. Gradually beat in the flour with the milk and egg into the yeast mixture. It will make a soft batter. Place the bowl in a warm place, cover lightly with waxed paper and let it stand overnight. In the morning bake the griddle cakes on a hot, greased griddle. Makes 16.

Quick and Easy

1½ cups milk
2 tbsps. melted butter **or** oil
2 tbsps. molasses

2 eggs
2 cups buckwheat flour
3 tsps. baking powder

Blend all the above ingredients together in a blender. DO NOT OVERBLEND. Bake on a hot greased griddle and serve with butter and molasses or honey.

Super-Instant

Make these delicious hot cakes up ahead of time. Stack them, separated, on sheets of wax paper. Heat in seconds on a hot, greased griddle.

Bran Supplement: Add ½ cup bran and ⅛ cup more milk.

Use rolled oats for this one—that is, those big flat flakes of oatmeal. By comparison those packaged "waffle mixes" taste like the stuff they use to put up wallpaper. (Incidentally, wallpaper paste *is* made from carefully refined white flour.)

Oatmeal-Nut Waffles—Traditional

SERVING TIME: 20–30 MINUTES

2 *cups milk*
2 *eggs*
1½ *cups whole-wheat pastry flour* **or** *stone-ground whole-wheat flour*
4 *tbsps. melted butter* **or** *oil*

2 *tsps. baking powder*
2 *tbsps. honey*
1 *cup rolled oats*
1 *cup chopped walnuts* **or** *pecans*

In a blender blend milk, eggs, flour, butter or oil, baking powder, and honey. Add the oatmeal and nuts. Mix well with a spoon. Bake in hot greased waffle iron. Serves 4–5.

Quick and Easy (SERVING TIME: 20 MINUTES)
Prepare the batter the night before. You're ready to go in the morning.

Super-Instant (SERVING TIME: 5 MINUTES)
These are easily made up ahead of time and frozen. They warm perfectly in your toaster, so they can constantly be ready for breakfasts or snacks for the kids.

🔥🔥

In these great waffles, the flavor and richness of the cornmeal comes through—it's kind of cornbread and waffle combined. We've never found anyone who didn't like it—although there's the possibility of a grouch in any neighborhood.

Corn Waffles—Traditional

SERVING TIME: 20–30 MINUTES

2 eggs
¼ cup oil
1½ cup milk

2 tbsps. honey or molasses
2 tsps. baking powder
1¾ cup cornmeal

Mix ingredients in a blender for 30 seconds or so. DON'T OVER-BLEND. Bake on waffle iron. Serve with honey or molasses. Makes 3 large rectangular waffles of 4 sections each. Serves 4.

Quick and Easy (SERVING TIME: 15 MINUTES)
The batter can be made the night before. In the morning all you need to do is cook it on the waffle iron.

Super-Instant (SERVING TIME: 3 MINUTES)
These waffles can be made up ahead of time and frozen. When you need them, just take out of the freezer, pop them into the toaster, and in a few minutes you're ready for a super treat.

Bran Supplement: Add ½ cup bran and ¼ cup more milk.

🐞 🐌

This is an excellent dough for any kind of fruit pie, meat pie, tart, and dishes like quiche Lorraine. It converts pastries from guilt-provoking no-no's into an important and nourishing part of the daily diet. When you think about it for a moment, there is really no reason why every pastry that tastes good also has to hurt your body. This high-fiber pie dough takes the pain from pleasure.

High-Fiber Pie Dough—Traditional

SERVING TIME: 10 MINUTES

2¼ cups whole-wheat pastry
flour

6 tbsps. butter, cold
6–8 tbsps. ice-cold water

In a mixing bowl put the flour. Take the cold butter and cut it into 8–10 pieces. With pastry blender or two knives, cut butter into the flour. You should end up with a crumbly-looking mixture, each crumb about the size of a pea. Gradually mix in the ice-cold water. Mix in only as much as will make a soft dough which just holds together. Place the dough on a waxed piece of paper and chill. After the dough is well chilled, lightly flour a board, cut the dough in half and roll out each half, being careful not to use too much flour or to handle the dough too much. Enough for one double-crust pie or two pie crusts.

Bran Supplement: Because of the nature of pie dough, it takes practice to roll out this dough with bran included, but try it. It's delicious. Add ½ cup bran.

🐦 🦅

It's really a travesty to call this "Armenian Pizza," because it's a million times better than pizza ever was. (Don't get excited until you taste it for yourself—then you can write those letters postmarked "Palermo.") Anyhow, we are giving it that name until America learns to pronounce "LAMADJoun" (LA-MA-JUNE . . . more or less). The dough is sensational, and after you roll it out in 8-inch discs, the mixture of meat and spices that goes on top transforms it into an experience you won't forget.

Armenian Pizza Lahmajoun—Traditional

SERVING TIME: 30–40 MINUTES

1 package yeast or 1 tbsp. yeast, dissolved in ¼ cup warm water with a ½ tsp. of honey. Let stand for a few minutes.

2 cups stone-ground whole-wheat flour (approx.)
1 cup bran
⅛ pound, or ¼ cup, butter, melted
¾–1 cup water

Prepare the yeast. Then place the flour and bran on a bread board. Make a hole in the middle and pour in the melted butter and begin to mix the flour into the butter. Then gradually add the water and yeast mixture, and continue mixing in the flour until you have a very soft, unsticky well-kneaded ball of dough. Put the dough in a greased bowl and cover with a towel. Let stand in a warm place until it has doubled in size. Punch down the dough and make about 12 egg-sized balls. Let them all stand a few minutes, then roll out each ball of dough to the size of an 8″ pancake. Place the rolled-out rounds on greased cookie sheets, cover with the meat mixture described in Chapter 6, and proceed with directions in the recipe.

Quick and Easy (SERVING TIME: 15 MINUTES)
These can be rolled and stacked, separated by layers of wax paper, in the morning, and then filled and cooked at night.

Super-Instant (SERVING TIME: 3–10 MINUTES)
The lahmajoun filled and cooked can also be stacked in between layers of wax paper and frozen, ready on any occasion . . . heat and serve, as they say, in a preheated 350-degree oven about 10 minutes, or under the broiler, carefully in 2–3 minutes.

🐟🦐

Chapatis are tortillas, East Indian style. The thinner the better, but don't worry about it, just as long as they cook through. Occasionally we run out of "masa," or cornmeal, and our cook, who is from El Salvador, has to make chapatis instead of tortillas. We see her shaking her head in disbelief, but she's a good-natured girl—and sometimes she even eats *one*. But we're sure you'll like them—at least 500 million people eat a few every day. You can put anything on a chapati that you'd put on bread—jam, meat, cheese, eggs, fish; let your taste be your guide.

Chapatis—Traditional

SERVING TIME: 20–30 MINUTES

1 cup bran
2 cups whole-wheat flour

⅛ pound butter
cold water (about ⅔ cup)

Put the bran and flour in a mixing bowl. Cut the butter into several pieces and blend into the flour using fingertips, a pastry blender, or two knives, until it has the consistency of bread crumbs. Gradually add the cold water, a little at a time, and work the dough until you have a soft, unsticky dough. Knead the dough at bit on a floured board. Divide the dough into 12 balls, about 1 inch in diameter. Roll each one into a thin round 5–6 inches in diameter and bake on a hot pancake griddle which has been brushed well with butter. Each side should be well browned, about a minute or two of cooking on each side.

Quick and Easy (SERVING TIME: 15–20 MINUTES)
Prepare the dough and the balls when you have a free moment, or the day before. Then the next day you only have to roll them out and cook them.

Super-Instant (SERVING TIME: 5–10 MINUTES)
Prepare and cook the chapatis ahead of time and stack them in tin foil. When you need them they can be warmed in a preheated 350-degree oven about 5 minutes, or heated on the griddle in seconds.

🌀🌀

A tortilla is the closest thing to a perfect slice of bread. Surprised? If we take a close look at these humble little discs, we see that they are nothing more than unleavened whole-grain cornbread—packed with vitamins, minerals, and, of course, fiber. That's one reason why Latin-Americans who grow up munching tortillas have much less tooth decay, colon cancer, and fewer heart attacks than their American counterparts. Of course, Americans grow up on balloon bread—stripped of fiber, loaded with sugar, and robbed of vitamins. (Those cheapy synthetic vitamins used to "enrich" the gloopy mess don't really count.) But, of course, the wrappers look nice. The basic ingredients in tortillas are only two: ground whole corn and lime water (fresh water with the added calcium of lime). Don't buy "instant masa" or any other product that makes instant tortillas. If you live in a big city, check the yellow pages for "Tortillas" and buy them *freshly made.* If you can't find them anywhere, ask the nearest Mexican, Puerto Rican, or other Latino grandmother. She'll help you find some, and if you give her a chance she'll tell you some other things about good eating you never suspected.

The Latin American diet makes the American diet look very bad by comparison. Consider it for a moment: high-fiber tortillas with natural vitamins and minerals plus protein, a bit of cheese or meat or sour cream to fill out the amino acid requirements, chili to add massive amounts of vitamin C, and plenty of fresh fruits and vegetables. And we thought we were so smart!

Tortillas—Traditional

SERVING TIME: 30 MINUTES

*1 pound masa (from Mexican
or Latin-American store)*

Wet your hands. Divide dough into 20–24 balls. Place one ball on a piece of waxed paper and pat flat between your hands while gradually turning the paper until you have a round tortilla about ¼ inch thick. Bake on a medium-hot lightly oiled griddle, turning several times until the tortilla is well cooked—each side will be a speckled golden brown. Depending on the heat and type of griddle you use, each tortilla takes about 2 minutes to cook.

Quick and Easy (SERVING TIME: 15–20 MINUTES)
Cook tortillas ahead of time, and heat on the griddle in a matter of seconds whenever you want. They will keep warm for about two hours if you wrap them in aluminum foil and then in several layers of newspaper.

6

Meat

Meat—tantalizing tasty chops, roasts, steaks, stews, and all the rest. There are few foods that should be more wholesome and health-giving than beef, lamb, pork, veal, and mutton. After all, the human race was designed and manufactured to eat meat. Just check your teeth—those sharp little ones three over from the center are canines, just perfect for tearing animal flesh. It makes good nutritional sense to include some meat in the daily diet. Meat is a good source of protein, some vitamins, some minerals, and trace elements and other nutrients. That's the good part.

The bad part is that U.S. meat is also a potential source of oxytetracycline, penicillin, progesterone, sulfa-chlorpyridazine, testosterone, tetracycline, tylosin, zeranol, diethylstilbesterol, arsenic, streptomycin, melangesterol acetate plus about 35 other prescription drugs. These are the chemicals banned in many other nations that American food processors are allowed to pump into the animals that you and your children are going to eat.

The only justification for the use of these chemicals—many of them obviously hazardous—is an economic one. They save money for meat producers. If you want to freak out on a 35-chemical cocktail, that's your business. But that kind of junk shouldn't be inflicted on everybody—especially against their will.

What can you do about it? You can try to buy your meat from someone you know—a small producer who promises not to dope up his animals in the hope of a few cents' more profit. (For example, the U.S. Department of Agriculture estimates that adding the proven cancer-causing chemical DES to beef saves the American consumer about three cents a pound. Based on the average yearly consumption of 122 pounds of beef a year, all the DES you gulp—and the hazard of cancer it brings—saves you—at the most—a big $4.27 annually. Now it gets a little clearer.

Until your elected representatives go to bat for you, there's not much you can do—except lower your intake of meat. There are two good reasons for that. First, excessive meat consumption —122 pounds a year—keeps you from eating enough high-fiber fruits, cereals, and vegetables. (Although meat does contain fibers, they are digestible animal fibers and do not provide any protection from the deadly diseases of civilization.) Another thing that eating less meat does is lower your exposure to the potentially deadly chemicals that lace American meat.

One other smart move might be to stay as far away as possible from any meat product cured with sodium nitrate and/or sodium nitrite. These are rigorously prohibited in most civilized countries —they are deadly poisonous chemicals and can combine with natural substances present in food and in the body to cause cancer. American food processors use them for one reason only: they combine with meat components to form red chemicals, nitrosomyoglobin and nitrosohemoglobin. That's what gives ham, bacon, sausage, smoked fish, and certain *baby foods* that bright red color. The risk of cancer is a big price to pay for reddish sausage. Meat packers protest that the amount of nitrates/nitrites in meat products is tiny, but that's not true. Even our look-the-other-way government allows a mere 500 parts per million of nitrates and 200 parts per million of nitrites in meats. The "meat people," in their own surveys, have found plenty of sausage and preserved meat that contain up to 40 percent more nitrate and 140 percent more nitrite than the maximum legal limits.* There have been cases of sausage containing 6,570 parts per million of nitrites or a mere 3,285 percent in excess of the lawful limit. The "meat people" try to justify the use of nitrates and nitrites on the ground that they prevent botulism in meat products. There are two things that they know but don't tell you. One, the use of these poisons to prevent botulism is not a legal use. Two, the real way to avoid botulism toxins in meat products is to observe sanitary procedures in the packing plants, plus sterilization and

* *Eater's Digest*, Michael Jacobson, Doubleday, 1972, p. 166.

refrigeration. Many foreign countries and some small American manufacturers avoid the use of nitrates and nitrites completely. So far, those who eat their products are just as healthy as nitrate/nitrite loaded citizens—maybe even healthier? Name-brand ham and bacon—aside from containing nitrate/nitrite—is generally abysmal in taste. Regrettably, few Americans have ever been given the opportunity to sample real naturally cured pork products. For about the last twenty-five years the big packers have turned out a "cured" ham in *seven minutes* (including, one supposes, ninety seconds or so for "aging"). Bacon—that may carry mouth-watering labels like "sugar-cured," "ranch-style," "down-home"—takes about *three minutes* to cure! Putting factory-made foods like that up for sale is insulting the intelligence of the American consumer.

Pork itself is an interesting situation. It is the one form of meat produced in America that you can eat with complete safety—if you live in another country. You see, it's like this:

There is an extremely dangerous parasite of pigs called trichinella spiralis, which causes a severe disease known as trichinosis in human beings who ingest infected pork. Americans consume an estimated 180,000 pounds of infected pork every week—that's 468 *tons* a year! A very small amount of pork is available which is certified to be trichinosis-free—but you'll never taste it. It is for export only, since many foreign countries refuse to admit any U.S. pork unless it is examined for this terrible infection. The children of countries like Germany, Austria, Italy, and France will never be infected with trichinosis from American pork—which is more than you can say for your kids.

Instead of insisting on sanitary pork production and processing, the U. S. Department of Agriculture takes TV spots to tell you to cook your pork well. That's like the city piping sewage-contaminated water to your home and advising you to boil it.

That leaves veal as a relatively uncontaminated meat—but most veal sold in the U. S. is elderly calf or "baby beef." The correct definition of "veal" is meat from a cow's offspring that has not been weaned.

All things considered, veal would *appear* to be the ideal meat. Since it comes from animals which have not been weaned, there is little opportunity for it to be doped with hazardous drugs—

except what it absorbs from its mother's milk. But try and find genuine veal in American markets. The meat labeled "veal" is usually nothing more than elderly calf, or what can be charitably described as "baby beef." Real veal has small bones, very pale pink meat, and almost no fat. It also starts at about $4 a pound and goes up from there.

What's the answer? There are rules of self-defense for eating in America and they are vital to your health. (What a tragedy that American families have to defend themselves against the poisons injected into this basic food product.) Here they are:

1. *Never* consume any meat product that contains poisonous nitrates or nitrites.
2. Do not knowingly consume—or feed to your family—any meat that you have reason to believe was treated with DES. Ironically, imported meat is likely to be safest in this regard.
3. Never eat pork unless it has been "thoroughly cooked." If you can get your hands on some pork destined for Italy, France, or some other country with rigorous sanitary requirements, you will be safe. The hazard is so great that even spreading butter with a knife that has been used to trim infected raw pork can sicken your entire family.
4. Until your elected officials protect you and your family from poisons and parasites in your meat, cut your meat consumption to a minimum. The less meat you eat, the less poison you absorb from the several dozen chemicals. America is the greatest country in the world, and American meat can be the greatest meat in the world. But until it is de-chemicalized, according to the opinion of your government officials, scientific experts, and the courts themselves, it can be hazardous to your health.

You will notice that most of the meat recipes which follow use relatively small amounts of meat and relatively large amounts of high-fiber ingredients. That cuts your exposure to meat-chemicals and increases your intake of dietary fiber. Besides, these are the tastiest recipes we could come up with. We hope you like them.

Recipes

This is a *real* Mexican recipe—not synthetic tacos this time. You cut down the amount of meat and increase the vegetables and fruit if you want to. Be sure and use good-quality vinegar. Wine vinegar is the best, and "distilled vinegar" is one of the worst. Actually, vinegar should taste good enough to eat by the spoonful. If it hits your tongue like a lightning bolt, keep looking.

Machaca—Traditional

SERVING TIME: 10–15 MINUTES

3 pounds brisket
2 tbsps. pickling spices
2 large onions, cut in half
½–1 cup vinegar, to taste
Freshly ground black pepper

Ground chili
4–6 avocados, cut in cubes
1 large head of lettuce, finely
   shredded, **or** about 2 pounds
   leaf lettuce, finely shredded

In a large pot or kettle put the brisket with pickling spices and onions. Cover with water, bring to a boil. Partially cover and simmer for 3¼–4 hours. The meat should string apart easily. When cooked take the meat out of the pot and let cool a bit. When it is not too hot to handle, string the meat—that is, break the brisket apart into stringlike pieces. Toss the meat with the vinegar and let stand for a while. Taste the meat. It should have a slightly vinegar taste, not too strong, but not too tame either. Add more vinegar if necessary, to taste. Toss the meat with the avocadoes and the lettuce. Sprinkle lots of freshly ground black pepper and the ground chili to taste. It should have a slightly piquant taste. Serve on lettuce leaves. Serves 6.

🌀🌀

The chalupa is the bacon-lettuce-and-tomato sandwich of Latin America. That is to say, it is the perfect combination of textures, flavors, and colors. It's also good for you. A modern BLT sandwich consisting of chemically cured, nitrate/nitrite loaded bacon, smeared with imitation mayonnaise, lying atop pesticide-baptized lettuce, and a tasteless tomato, all in a coffin of gloopy fiberless white "bread" is a nutritional disaster area.

For a great taste combination, put the chapatis or tortillas in the oven—350 degrees—long enough to make them crispy. Wow! I can taste them now! . . .

Beef Chalupas—Traditional

SERVING TIME: 15–20 MINUTES

2 pounds brisket **or** 3 cups leftover meat, chopped
2 onions
1 tsp. freshly ground black pepper
¼ cup vinegar
1 tbsp. pickling spices
1 large head lettuce, finely shredded
2 green peppers, finely sliced
3 tomatoes, chopped
1 medium onion, finely sliced

4–5 springs Chinese parsley (cilantro) **or** 4–5 sprigs regular parsley and 2 tsps. ground coriander seed and 1 tsp. chervil and 2 tsps. crushed oregano
⅓ cup oil
⅓ cup vinegar
Freshly ground black pepper
3 cups mashed beans (p. 115)
12 tortillas or chapatis

Put the brisket in a large pot and cover with water. Add 2 onions, cut in half, 1 teaspoon freshly ground black pepper, ¼ cup vinegar, and 1 tablespoon pickling spices. Cook the brisket several hours until it is soft and the meat falls apart fairly easily. (When you know that you want to make chalupas, it is a good idea to cook the meat at night or in the morning. Then it is ready to be pulled apart into stringlike pieces.) In a salad bowl put the lettuce, green pepper, tomatoes, onion, Chinese parsley or the regular parsley mixed with the coriander, chervil, and oregano. Mix well with oil and vinegar and freshly ground black pepper. Heat mashed beans. Lay out the tortillas. Spread ¼ cup of the mashed beans on each tortilla. On top put about ½ cup of the stringed meat. Cover generously with several heaping spoonfuls of salad. Put 2 chalupas on each plate. Serves 6.

"Picadillo" is pretty much untranslatable—the best I can do is "little cut-up things." But the flavor is universal. Wholehearted spices, raisins, olives, nuts—serve it with tortillas or chapatis, and you get meat flavor with high-fiber protection: the best of both worlds.

Picadillo—Traditional

SERVING TIME: 10 MINUTES

2 tbsps. olive oil
3 large onions, chopped
2–3 cloves garlic, minced
4 pounds ground meat (combination of pork and beef is best)
5 cups liquefied tomatoes (approx. 5 medium tomatoes in blender)
½ cup chopped small hot green chilis, or 2–3 tbsps. ground chili (New Mexico style)

½ cup chopped nuts (almonds, walnuts, or pecans)
½ cup seedless raisins
½ cup sliced, pitted black olives
2 tbsps. cinnamon
½ tsp. cloves
2 tbsps. crushed cumin seeds
¼ cup chopped parsley
1 tsp. freshly ground black pepper

In a large frying pan sauté the onions and garlic in the oil about one minute. Add the meat and fry it until it loses color, stirring frequently. Add tomatoes, liquefied, either fresh chilis or ground chili, nuts, raisins, black olives, cinnamon, cloves, cumin, parsley, and black pepper, and simmer about 20–30 minutes so that the flavors will blend, stirring occasionally. Spoon off fat from surface. This is another dish which is better the second and third days, because of the melding of flavors. Serve with tortillas or chapatis on the side, or as a filling like tacos. Serves 8.

ᘏᘍ

"Olla de carne" means "a big pot of meat," but it really turns out to be a big pot of sumptuous vegetables with some meat thrown in. Serve with the broth, which is loaded with minerals from the meat, vegetables, and spices. There is a lot of fiber in every plateful plus the simple elegance of the basic country-style dish. By the way, that's a *head* of garlic, not a *clove*; you can cut it down if you want to, but we think you'll like it that way. For those who don't like garlic, see the special note: "A Word About Garlic" (p. 23).

Olla de Carne—Traditional

SERVING TIME: 10 MINUTES

2 *pounds brisket or stew meat*
1 *head of garlic cut in half crosswise and put in pot with skin, for flavor*
1 *tsp. freshly ground black pepper*
1 *tbsp. marjoram*
3 *large onions, cut in half*
6 *small potatoes with skins, scrubbed*

3 *large beets, scrubbed and cut in quarters*
3 *turnips, scrubbed and cut in quarters*
6 *carrots, scrubbed and cut in half*
1 *large cabbage, cut in wedges*
3 *chayote, peeled and cut in half* **or** *3 zucchini or summer squash scrubbed and cut in thirds*

In a large kettle or soup pot, about 8–10 quarts, put the meat, garlic, black pepper, marjoram, and onions. Cover with water, bring to a boil, then cover pot and simmer about 2 hours. Then add all the rest of the ingredients and add more water if necessary to cover about two thirds. Cover and simmer another hour and a half. Serves 6–8.

🔥🔥

Chorizo—Traditional
SERVING TIME: 15–20 MINUTES

2 pounds lean pork
½ pound pork fat
1 green or red sweet pepper
1 large onion
¼ cup vinegar
1 tsp. cinnamon

3–4 cloves garlic
1 tbsp. crushed cumin seeds
1 tbsp. crushed oregano
2–4 tbsps. ground chili (3
    tbsps. makes the chorizo
    moderately picante)

Grind the pork, pork fat, sweet pepper, and onion together. Add vinegar and spices. Mix well. Store in refrigerator, well sealed. If you don't have a grinder, ask the butcher to grind a piece of pork which you pick. Mince the onion and green pepper in the blender and finely dice the pork fat by hand. Mix together well. If you want to make individual sausages, buy 7½ to 8 feet of casings. It is better to hand-dice the fat when you are going to stuff casings. You can buy the natural casings from your butcher. Makes 5 cups sausage meat or 10 4-ounce patties.

Chorizo is used more for seasoning than anything else—you won't be frying up a couple of pounds to eat for breakfast with greasy eggs. You will be imparting a pork-and-spice flavor to the recipes that require this delightful sausage. At the same time, you have sausage at laughably low prices with much more meat and less fat than any commercial sausage ever made. The big bonus is the one that matters most: *no chemicals!* The natural sausage casings are really an afterthought. There's no real necessity to put the filling into casings unless you particularly like the idea. And, of course, with U.S. pork, wash your utensils thoroughly after using, and cook the sausage well.

🔥🔥

For dedicated meat lovers, this might be described as "meat-on-meat." But you'll notice that lurking in the shadows is enough

bran to make it all worthwhile. Like the recipe says, don't be
afraid to make it the day before—it can only get better.

Flank Steak Stuffed with Chorizo—Traditional

SERVING TIME: 15 MINUTES

*1 pound chorizo. If you can't
find this Spanish sausage
without nitrates and nitrites,
see previous recipe or use
the following for a quick
substitution:
1 pound ground pork mixed
with ½ tsp. black pepper,
¼ tsp. nutmeg, ¼ tsp.
crushed hot peppers, 2 tsps.
crushed cumin seeds
2 bunches green onions,
chopped
¼ cup chopped parsley
1 cup finely chopped nuts
(walnuts, pecans, or
almonds)*

*1–3 tsps. ground chili to taste
(I use 3 tsps. and sometimes
a bit more)
2 eggs
¾ cup bran
2 1½–2-pound flank steaks
4 cloves garlic, minced
1 tbsp. olive oil
4 tomatoes, liquefied in
blender
1½ cups beef stock
1 bay leaf
1 tbsp. ginger
Juice of half a lemon*

Mix chorizo or ground pork and spices with green onions, parsley,
nuts, ground chili, eggs, and bran. Spread half the minced garlic
on one flank steak and half on the other. Fill each flank steak
with half the stuffing. Roll carefully and tie each roll in several
places. Fasten twice around its width and then once around its
length, folding the ends in to keep the filling from coming out.
In a large pot heat the oil and brown the two stuffed steaks. Add
the liquefied tomatoes, stock, bay leaf, ginger, and lemon juice.
Bake in preheated 350-degree oven for 1½ hours. Serves 6.
This dish gets better with age, so you can cook it the night before
and reheat the next day, and the result will be a superb blending
of flavors.

🌀🌀

If you can get real lamb in the United States, you're in luck. By definition, an animal of the sheep clan that is under 365 days old is a lamb. Anything older is adolescent mutton. Some of the meat marked "lamb" is going on two years old, but it may be all right. Lambs, by the way, are little animals—look for the miniature-size cuts. And Australian lamb is DES free.

Incidentally, chopping onions in a blender is really nifty. No crying, no slicing fingers. Just cut the peeled onions in quarters, drop in the blender, fill with cold water, *cover*, and turn the motor on and off a couple of times. Pour through a strainer, and you're in business. Works for cabbage, green peppers, ginger, and some other things you'll discover on your own.

High-Fiber Lamburgers (Kibbi)— Traditional

SERVING TIME: 10 MINUTES

2 cups bulghur (cracked wheat, the finer the better)

3 pounds ground lamb, beef, or pork (Lamb is preferable, and have the butcher grind the meat twice so that it is very fine)

2 onions, minced in blender

2 green peppers, minced in blender

¼ cup parsley, minced

½ tsp. freshly ground black pepper

2 tsps. cinnamon

2 tsps. allspice

2 tsps. ground chili

Soak the bulghur a few minutes in water while you are preparing the other ingredients. Then drain the bulghur and add to the meat with the minced vegetables and spices. Mix all in your mixer, or knead it by hand, until it has the consistency of dough. Add small amounts of cold water as you are kneading the moist dough, if needed. Shape into hamburger patties and fry in a very small amount of oil (1 tbsp.) or bake in preheated 400-degree oven on greased pans about 20 minutes. Makes 16 ½-cup patties. Serves 8.

🔥🔥

Country people in Balkan countries eat this dish first thing in the morning, and then climb mountains and hunt bears. That might make it just the thing for the young corporate executive on the way up. It's also full of fiber and tastes great. This is a dish that can be put on the stove early in the morning and left to cool on its own all day long.

Keskeg—Traditional

SERVING TIME: 20 MINUTES

1½ cups barley
4½ quarts beef stock
2 pounds beef, pork, or lamb
　(brisket or equivalent)
Freshly ground pepper (2 tsps.)

¼ cup melted butter
Ground chili
Ground cumin
Yogurt if desired

In a 6–8 quart pot put barley, stock, meat and about 2 teaspoons of black pepper. Bring to boil, lower heat, cover and simmer all day. Check the pot once or twice to see if there is enough liquid. If not, add more stock. Halfway through the cooking time remove meat, finely shred, and return to pot. The Middle Easterners like to beat this until it becomes mush. This is not necessary because it is so delicious as it is. Skim fat off surface. Melt the butter, mix in about ⅛ teaspoon black pepper per portion, about ¼ teaspoon of the chili per portion, and ½ teaspoon of the cumin per portion. Pour a little of this over each individual plateful. Many Middle Easterners also like to top the keskeg with dollops of yogurt. Try it both ways. Serves 6.

🔥🔥

Folks who taste lahmajoun for the first time have been known to put away a dozen helpings at one time. Keep every ingredient as fresh as possible—including the crushed peppers and mint, if

you can. The vitamin and mineral content will be very high, and
the fiber level superb. And remember, fresh lemon juice. The
bottled kind might be something made from lemon rind oil, lye,
propylene glycol, a shot of lemon juice, and a preservative. Just
have one of the kids squeeze a lemon—they might even need
the exercise.

Lahmajoun Meat Mixture—Traditional

SERVING TIME: 20–30 MINUTES

2 recipes of Lahmajoun dough
  for 24 rounds
2½ pounds ground lamb (You
  can use beef or pork or any
  combination, but the traditional uses lamb and it's
  delicious.)
3 cups onion, minced (in
  blender)
3 green peppers, minced (in
  blender)

2 cloves garlic, minced
Juice of half a lemon
¼ cup chopped fresh mint **or**
  1 tbsp. crushed dried mint
½ tsp. freshly ground black
  pepper
2 tsps. ground chili **or** ¼–½
  tsp. crushed hot peppers
8 small tomatoes, or about
  1½ cups (liquefied in
  blender

Prepare lahmajoun dough. Mix all the above ingredients together,
except the dough. Mix well. Roll out the dough rounds, spread
with the meat mixture and place on greased pans. Bake them in
a preheated 450-degree oven 15–20 minutes. These may be stacked
meat-side to meat-side in a large pot with a cover. Or they can
be stacked meat-side up on sheets of wax paper and stored in
the refrigerator for a few days until you need them.

Quick and Easy (SERVING TIME: 10–15 MINUTES)
Use slices of your whole-wheat bread. Spread the meat mixture on
the bread and bake in oven as above. This is delicious for a fast
snack.

🥀 🥀

Cook the lamb well—American lamb may be infected with echinococcus parasites, so rare lamb is out of the question. This is meat plus fiber, and is a wonderful combination of flavors. If I didn't have to finish this chapter, I'd go downstairs and eat some right now. I have to wait until later—but you don't.

Keufta—Traditional

SERVING TIME: 30–40 MINUTES

Outer layer:

2 pounds lean twice-ground lamb (You can use beef or pork or a combination, but the meat should be lean. Lamb is the traditional meat.)

3 cups medium to fine cracked wheat

1 large onion, minced in blender

¼ cup parsley, minced in blender

½ tsp. freshly ground black pepper

1 tsp. cinnamon, and 1 tsp. allspice (If you don't like these spices in meat, leave them out. This is delicious either way. Use instead 1 tsp. oregano and 1 tsp. dried mint.)

Filling:

2 tbsps. butter

½ cup pine nuts (or almonds, walnuts, or pecans—pine nuts are traditional)

3 large onions, chopped

1 medium green pepper, chopped

1½ pounds ground lamb (Use the same kind of meat or meat combination as you used for the outer layer.)

¼ cup chopped parsley

½ cup raisins

1 tsp. freshly ground black pepper

1 tbsp. cinnamon, and 1 tbsp. allspice (If you don't use these spices, try 1 tbsp. dried mint and 1 tbsp. oregano, and leave out the raisins.)

¼ tsp. crushed hot peppers

In skillet, sauté the pine nuts in the butter a few minutes until they become a golden brown. Add onions and green pepper, and sauté until the onions become transparent. Add lamb and sauté. When meat browns a bit, add the rest of the ingredients. Let the lamb cook 15–20 minutes while you are preparing the outer layer. The lamb must cook well. Stir every few minutes.

Outer layer:
Cover the cracked wheat with water and let stand while you mince the onion and parsley. In a large bowl or on a board put the meat with the minced onion and parsley and spices. Drain the cracked wheat and add it to the meat. Knead the combination well, adding sprinkles of cold water when needed to make a smooth meat dough. This takes about 15–20 minutes if done by hand. It can also be kneaded in your mixer. When you have a nice soft smooth meat dough, you are ready to put the keufta together. Preheat oven to 400 degrees.

Assembly:
In a large buttered rectangular baking pan, approximately 13 x 8 inches, put about one third of the outer layer mixture, spreading it evenly and wetting your hand with cold water from time to time as you are spreading it to keep the mixture from sticking to your hand and to help you spread it more evenly. On this bottom layer spread the meat filling. Spread the rest of the outer layer mixture on top, wetting hands to help spread the mixture evenly and smoothly. Score the top layer into diamond-shaped pieces about every 2 inches. Spoon 2–3 tablespoons of melted butter over the top. Bake in preheated 400-degree oven for 25–30 minutes; then lower heat to 325 degrees and bake for 30 minutes more. The keufta should be a golden brown on top. Serves 8.

Quick and Easy (SERVING TIME: 15 MINUTES)
This dish does not have to be prepared in one operation. Prepare and cook the filling in advance. Preparing the outer layer and assembling takes very little time. Use your mixer to save time, kneading the outer meat-and-cracked-wheat mixture. Don't forget to add sprinkles of cold water to make a smoother meat dough.

Piroshky are little packets of dough filled with flavorful mixes of meats or vegetables and spices. They exist in many lands under many names: empanadas, won ton, knishes. We like the Russian version because it is particularly hearty. The 100-percent whole-wheat dough makes it really high fiber. It's really good—the Czars ate it, the Boyars ate it, the Communists eat it—and we think you'll want to eat it. The Czars ate it, and the Communists eat it, and the only political issue ever involved in piroshky has been: "Who gets a second helping first?" Make plenty—they're just as good the second and third day, *if* there's any left.

Piroshky—Traditional

SERVING TIME: 45 MINUTES TO 1 HOUR

Dough:
2 packages yeast or 2 tbsps.
  yeast dissolved in ½ cup
  warm water and 1 tbsp.
  honey. Let stand a few
  minutes. It will rise.
5½–6½ cups stone-ground
  whole-wheat flour

1 cup bran
4 eggs
½ cup melted butter
1 cup milk

Prepare the yeast. On a board or counter put 4 cups of flour and the bran. Make a hole in the center and gradually work in the eggs. When the yeast mixture is ready, add it, the melted butter, and the milk, working in more and more flour. Add only as much flour as you need to make a soft, unsticky dough. Knead the dough well, 15–20 minutes. Place in a large greased bowl, cover with a towel, and let rise in a warm place until double in bulk (about 2 hours.) If you have a mixer with a dough hook, the mixer can knead the dough. This takes from 5–7 minutes.

Meat Filling:
2 tbsps. butter
4 cloves garlic, minced
4 large onions, minced (in blender)
2 pounds ground beef
4 carrots, minced (in blender)

½ cup parsley, minced (in blender)
½ cup fresh dill, minced (in blender)
8 hard-boiled eggs, chopped
1 tbsp. freshly ground black pepper

In a large frying pan sauté garlic and onions in butter for a minute or so. Add beef, and sauté until meat loses its redness. Mix in the rest of the ingredients and let filling cool just a bit. Drain liquid.

Cabbage Filling:
3 tbsps. butter
4 large onions, minced (in blender)
3 green peppers, minced (in blender)
2 medium cabbages, about 3 pounds, chopped

4 carrots, minced (in blender)
½ cup parsley, minced (in blender)
½ cup fresh dill, minced (in blender)
8 hard-boiled eggs, chopped
1 tbsp. freshly ground black pepper

In a large frying pan sauté onions and green peppers in the butter for a minute or so. Add the cabbage and carrots, and sauté another 2–3 minutes. Mix in the rest of the ingredients. Mix well. Let cool. Drain liquid.

Assembly:
Punch down dough. Take a piece of dough and, on floured board or counter, roll out to ⅛-inch thickness. Cut circles of dough about 3½–4 inches in diameter. Put a couple of tablespoons of filling on one round, moisten edge with a little water, and cover with another round, sealing the edges by pinching them together firmly. Or put filling on half the round, and fold over, sealing the edges with your fingers. Place the piroshky on greased pans, and let them rise, covered with a dishcloth, about an hour. Brush pies with beaten egg, milk, or melted butter. Bake in preheated 400-

degree oven about 15 minutes, or until a golden brown. Makes 64–68 rounds 3½ inches in diameter.

🌸🌸

The Chinese have been in the gourmet-cooking business for a long time—about 7000 years, more or less—and they have it down pat. Notice the high proportion of vegetables in their meat dishes—and you see that they had the high-fiber idea long ago. Vegetables should be fresh. The sauces—soy and oyster—are optional. They may contain sodium benzoate as a preservative which isn't an exciting idea—but there are no substitutes for their flavors, so that's a personal decision.

Pork or Beef with Vegetables, Chinese Style— Traditional

SERVING TIME: 15–20 MINUTES

2 tbsps. oil
2 cloves garlic, minced
1½ pounds pork or beef (beef flank steak is good) cut in ½-inch pieces
3 onions, sliced
4 carrots, cut into thin rounds or on an angle

2 green peppers, coarsely chopped
1 bunch fresh broccoli, trimmed and cut into small pieces
½ cup beef or chicken stock
2 tbsps. soy sauce
3 tbsps. molasses
2 tbsps. Chinese oyster sauce

In a large frying pan over high heat stir-fry the garlic in oil for a few seconds. Add the pork or beef, and stir-fry 4–7 minutes until the meat browns and cooks. Add onions, carrots, and green peppers, and stir-fry another couple of minutes. Add broccoli, stock, soy sauce, molasses, and oyster sauce. Stir well, cover and simmer for 5–8 minutes. Serves 6.

🦚🦜

Pork and cabbage love each other—onions and garlic should always be present at the wedding. As far as the rice is concerned, remember that until very recently in Chinese history, all Chinese rice was brown rice. That miserable ice-cream scoop of blazing-white soggy starch served in "Chinese" restaurants would have impelled the Emperors of China to lop off the heads of those responsible. That reminds me of the story of the impulsive Roman Emperor who was dissatisfied with one of his dinners. He thereupon ordered his soldiers to cook the cook and bake the baker. Hmmm . . . what should we do to the food processors?

Pork with Cabbage, Chinese Style—Traditional

SERVING TIME: 15–20 MINUTES

1 tbsp. oil
2 cloves garlic, minced
1 tbsp. minced fresh ginger
1½ pounds pork cut in match sticks, tiny bits or ground (preferably in match sticks)
3 large onions, chopped

1 bunch green onions, chopped
1 large head of cabbage, coarsely chopped
½ cup chicken stock
1 tbsp. soy sauce
2 tbsps. molasses
1 tbsp. Chinese sesame oil (optional but superb)

In a large frying pan over high heat stir-fry the garlic and ginger in the oil for a few seconds. Add the pork and stir-fry until pork cooks through. This takes 2–3 minutes. Add the onions and green onions, and continue stir-frying a minute or so. Add the cabbage, and stir-fry another couple of minutes. Add the stock, the soy sauce, and molasses, and stir well. Cover and simmer about 5 minutes. Uncover, stir in the sesame oil, and serve over or at the side of brown rice. Serves 6.

🏵️ 🏵️

Another Chinese success! You'll probably have to settle for canned bamboo shoots and water chestnuts, but you shouldn't use anything but home-grown bean sprouts. Use mung beans, and it will make a wonderful difference. Regular molasses is fine— you don't need the very expensive Oriental molasses. However, get the kind that doesn't have sulfur dioxide slugged into it. A final word—cook the pork well to zap those little killers the swine-herder may have left in there.

Beef or Pork with Bean Sprouts—Traditional

SERVING TIME: 15–20 MINUTES

1 tbsp. oil
2 cloves garlic, minced
2 bunches green onions, chopped
1½ pounds pork or beef, cut in thin sticks or ground
6 cups bean sprouts
8–10 Chinese mushrooms, sliced, soaked in warm water for 10 minutes, and drained

½ cup bamboo shoots
½ cup sliced water chestnuts
3 carrots, cut in rounds
2 tbsps. soy sauce
2 tbsps. molasses
1 tbsp. Chinese sesame oil (optional but worth keeping on hand)

In a large frying pan over high heat stir-fry the garlic and green onions in the oil for a few seconds. Add the pork or beef and continue stir-frying a few minutes until the meat is cooked. Add the bean sprouts, the Chinese mushrooms, the already-soaked-and-sliced bamboo shoots, water chestnuts, carrots, soy sauce, and molasses. Continue stir-frying another 3–5 minutes. Add sesame oil, stir well, and serve. Serves 6.

🏵️ 🏵️

A few key points: Use fresh pineapple and fresh ginger if you can. Cook the pork thoroughly, but don't overcook the rest of the ingredients. Really, all you want to do is heat up the vegetables. Same rules apply to soy sauce: they got you. If you want the taste, you have to use the processed version.

Sweet and Sour Pork with Vegetables—Traditional

SERVING TIME: 15–20 MINUTES

2 *pounds pork, cut in ½-inch*
   cubes
1 *tbsp. soy sauce*
1 *tbsp. minced fresh ginger*
2 *tbsps. salad oil*
2 *onions, chopped*
2 *bunches green onions,*
   chopped
3 *green peppers, coarsely*
   chopped

3 *carrots, cut in rounds*
3 *tomatoes, coarsely chopped*
1 *medium cabbage, shredded*
1 *pound fresh pineapple, bite-*
   size chunks
3 *tbsps. molasses*
3 *tbsps. vinegar*
1 *tbsp. soy sauce*

Toss the pork cubes with the 1 tablespoon soy sauce and fresh ginger, and let stand while you prepare the other vegetables. In the oil over high heat in a large frying pan stir-fry the pork cubes until they are cooked. This will take 5–10 minutes. Then add the onions, green onions, green peppers, and carrots, and stir-fry another minute. Add the tomatoes, and stir-fry another minute. Add the cabbage and stir-fry another minute or slightly longer, until the cabbage begins to wilt just a bit. Add the pineapple, molasses, vinegar, and soy sauce. Stir-fry everything together another 3–4 minutes. Serves 6.

🔥🔥

Remember, "Madras curry" is not a brand name, just like "miller's bran" is not a brand name. It just tells what kind of curry it is. Buy the best curry you can find, and it will prove its value. Never use that stringy, gooey processed coconut—it is replete with chemicals and sugar. Put a little fresh coconut in a blender, and you'll see what we mean. (If you have any shredded coconut left over, just mix it with a little honey, and there's a super dessert.)

Meat-Vegetable Curry—Traditional

SERVING TIME: 15–20 MINUTES

2 tbsps. butter
2 large onions, chopped
2 green peppers, chopped
1 small cauliflower, chopped
2 pounds beef, pork, or lamb, cut in ½-inch cubes or ground
2 carrots, cut in rounds
1 cup fresh peas

1 cup fresh green beans, cut in thirds
1 zucchini or summer squash, diced
1 cup beef or chicken stock
2 tbsps. Madras curry
½ cup half and half
1 cup fresh coconut, grated (in blender), optional

In a large frying pan over high heat cook the onions and green peppers in butter for a minute or so. Add the meat and sauté some more, about 3–5 minutes. Add the cauliflower and continue sautéeing another minute or two. Add the rest of the vegetables, stock, and curry, and simmer, covered, about 15 minutes. Uncover, add half and half and grated coconut. Simmer another couple of minutes. Serve with rice. Serves 6.

7
Poultry & Fish

The United States has come a long way from the time when "chicken every Sunday" was a major national goal. The cost of chicken has steadily declined (except for recent inflationary price increases). Unfortunately, the quality has followed the price down. Years ago, most chickens were raised by "Mom and Pop" chicken "farmers," and grew up under natural conditions, and were fattened on corn. Nowadays, most chickens live in monstrous penitentiaries, jammed together under horrendous conditions for their short lives. They are dosed on antibiotics to suppress the diseases that overcrowding produces, and gorged on such unexciting additives as arsenic, adrenalin, and sodium iodoacetate. You can still find chickens with nice yellow fat—that kind that comes from eating corn—only, these days it's probably a result of feeding the poultry something called "tagates meal." (Tagates meal is ground-up marigold flowers.)

One sometimes gets the feeling that if the food-processing companies could find a way to make a cheap *plastic* chicken, they would. Then they'd hire a Madison Avenue outfit to tell us how much better it was for our health to feast on Prefabricated Poultry. In any event, purchasing poultry is a matter of self-defense these days. Try your very best to find a poultry raiser in your area who treats his chickens like potential food for human beings, instead of feathered chemistry sets. Buy from him—even if it costs more. If you can't do that, try to get fresh chickens—not frozen corpses which may have been slaughtered months ago. There is even a little ethnic wrinkle that may come in handy: In some large American cities there are "kosher" chicken markets where live chickens are kept. You go in, pick out your chicken, and the (usually) elderly gentleman kills it, plucks it, and cleans it right on the spot. That's about the only way for city people to get anything approaching fresh poultry these days. If you get your chicken at the supermarket, open the plastic shroud it comes in before you leave the store—and smell it. It should smell *good*. If it doesn't, keep opening shrouds until you find one that does.

Chicken goes well with high-fiber recipes, since a relatively small amount of chicken meat adds a lot of flavor. In countries with natural high-fiber diets, chicken is a big favorite—chicken tacos, Chinese chicken dishes, and the like. Incidentally, most of these poultry recipes are interchangeable—if you find a good buy in turkey, you can use it instead of chicken.

Now let us move, mournfully, to the subject of fish. Fish—and seafood in general—is a highly desirable part of the human diet. Relatively inexpensive (except for *prestige* seafood like shrimp, oysters, and lobster), wholesome, and a good companion for high-fiber foods, it should make all the dietary sense in the world. But fish eaters these days take all kinds of big risks. Let's consider first the question of mercury. Because manufacturing plants along the coast have dumped mercury-containing wastes into the oceans, tiny marine animals have become contaminated with the poisonous metal. Fish eat these tiny animals and absorb the mercury into their own bodies. (Incidentally, this is *not* the kind of silvery mercury you see in fever thermometers—it is methyl-mercury, *an extremely toxic organic compound.*) In the late 1960's and early 1970's scientists discovered methyl-mercury in fish for human consumption. Some fish, like blue-fin tuna and swordfish, had more than half a milligram per two pounds or so. Seventy milligrams is the fatal dose of methyl-mercury, so about 140 pounds of swordfish or blue-fin tuna will send you to your great reward. Of course, no one is going to eat that in one sitting—but it's conceivable that tuna-loving Americans might eat that much in a year—and there's a little catch: methyl-mercury is not efficiently eliminated from the body; it tends to accumulate for life. It can cause convulsions and progressive brain damage. Since the poison is transmitted to unborn infants and concentrates in their brains, it is an extremely dangerous chemical for helpless fetuses.

Methyl-mercury can kill outright. A number of Japanese were wiped out when they consumed mercury-contaminated fish near a mercury-using plant in Japan. Unfortunately, once the mercury gets into the ocean, there's no way to get it out. The fish continue to be exposed to it, and it accumulates in their flesh.

Now let's look at the hard facts. After the initial revelation that Americans were consuming fish contaminated with poison mercury, consumption of fish declined drastically. That caused large financial losses for the fishing industry, and a public relations campaign was swiftly mounted. The basic theme was "Now the mercury scare is over!" Such exciting examples were cited as the discovery that preserved fish specimens in museums were found to contain mercury and, besides, a person had to eat a lot of fish to run any risks. Other contamination stories, like Watergate, began to take over the headlines, and Americans by the millions started eating fish again. For them, the fish scare was over. But knowledgeable scientists are still scared. What worries them are things like this:

1. Tuna and swordfish still contain mercury.
2. Fish like trout, bass, perch, and other species may also contain mercury.
3. For many years the U.S. government insisted that the safe level of mercury in fish was *zero; no mercury at all in any amount whatsoever was considered safe for human consumption.*
4. Suddenly, after December 30, 1970, the U. S. Department of Health, Education, and Welfare decided that the safe level of mercury, *as if by magic*, had risen to half a milligram per kilogram (2.2 pounds)!

In a stunning decision, right out of science fiction ("Doublethink"), the U.S. government decided that the *safe level of a poisonous substance* (which had previously been totally *excluded* from a food product) instantly coincided with the actual level of contamination! To make the whole business even more weird, they justified it by saying that Americans don't eat a lot of fish anyway! Where does that leave the poor Americans who *do* eat a lot of fish?

The fact is that the mercury is still there and if you consume it, it's your own risk. (To fortify yourself against "The scare is over!" boys, a list of current references is included below.)

Nevertheless there are *some folks* who are still going to eat fish. Hopefully they will eat fresh-caught fish from little mountain streams. Others will fish uncontaminated lakes, rivers, and ponds —although these are getting harder to find every day. And a few are just stubborn and will eat anything that doesn't make them keel over before they finish chewing it. So here are some fish recipes designed to encourage the consumption of high-fiber items along with zero-fiber fish. Good luck!

Mercury-In-Fish References:
  Henderson, C., et al., "Mercury Levels In Fish, 1969–1970," *Pesticides Monitoring Journal*, 6:144–150, 1972.
  Novick, S., "A New Pollution Problem: Federal Official Comment," *Environment*, 11:8, 1969.

Recipes

Chicken loves lemon, barley loves lemon, chicken loves barley—a gastronomical triangle. You'll fall in love with it, too. One big problem with pasty, mushy low-fiber cooking is that it all ends up tasting the same. But each high-fiber dish has a lasting character of its own. This recipe is no exception.

Roast Chicken with Barley Stuffing—Traditional

SERVING TIME: 20–30 MINUTES

2 3–3½ pound whole chickens	2 tbsps. olive oil
4 lemons	Freshly ground black pepper
1 head of garlic, minced	Barley stuffing (p. 49)

Wash and dry the chickens. Squeeze the lemons. If you don't want to mince the garlic by hand, put the lemon juice, peeled garlic, and olive oil into the blender and blend at high speed for a few seconds. Rub this lemon-garlic mixture inside and outside the chickens. Sprinkle the chickens with freshly ground black pepper, to taste. Stuff the chickens with the barley stuffing. Sew the ends closed or use thin skewers for fastening them. Lay the stuffed chickens on their sides on racks in a shallow roasting pan and roast, uncovered, in a preheated 400-degree oven for 15 minutes. Then lower heat to 350 degrees and roast about an hour. If you like the chicken very crispy on top, leave in just a little longer. When it is crispy on one side, turn it over to allow the other side to crisp. Serves 6–8.

🌀🌀

Pineapple, ginger, vinegar: all acid flavors that make the chicken vibrant and appealing! Cook fast at high heat and you'll be glad you did.

Spicy Pineapple Chicken—Traditional

SERVING TIME: 20–25 MINUTES

2 tbsps. oil
2 cloves garlic, minced
2 bunches green onions, sliced
1–2 tbsps. fresh ginger, minced
2 pounds chicken breasts,
   boned and thinly sliced into
   julienne strips
3 green peppers, chopped
2 cups chopped celery

4 carrots, cut in thin rounds
2 tomatoes, chopped
2 cups shredded cabbage
2 cups fresh pineapple, cut in
   chunks
1 tbsp. soy sauce
3 tbsps. molasses
3 tbsps. vinegar

In a large frying pan over high heat stir-fry garlic, green onions, and ginger for a few seconds. Add chicken and stir-fry about 5 minutes until chicken cooks. Add green peppers, celery, carrots, and tomatoes, and stir-fry another minute or so. Add cabbage and stir-fry another minute. Add pineapple, soy sauce, molasses, and vinegar. Stir-fry another 2–3 minutes and serve. Serves 6.

🐟🐟

This recipe should be made with *real* horseradish—actually a very simple dish. Just take a piece of horseradish, peel it with a potato peeler, cut it into small chunks, put it in the blender, add some wine vinegar, and blend. Let the fumes disperse, and there you are! That junk in the little jars will never appeal to you again.

Chicken Stuffed with Kasha—Traditional

SERVING TIME: 20–30 MINUTES

1½ cups buckwheat groats, whole or split, to be cooked in 4½ cups chicken stock **or** *6 cups cooked buckwheat (kasha)*
6 portions chicken breasts (3 whole breasts, halved)
Juice of 2 lemons
Freshly ground black pepper
1 cup water
2 tbsps. butter
2 large onions, chopped
½ cup chopped green pepper

¼ pound mushrooms, sliced
½ cup carrots, shredded in blender
2 cups cabbage, shredded in blender
1 cup finely diced zucchini squash or summer squash (with skin)
1 cup chicken stock
1 cup sour cream
1–2 tbsps. minced horseradish, to taste

In a saucepan put the buckwheat groats in the 4½ cups chicken stock. Bring to a boil, lower heat, and simmer, covered, about 20 minutes, or until the broth is absorbed. Rub the chicken breasts with lemon juice. In a large frying pan place the chicken breasts, sprinkle freshly ground black pepper on them, add ¼ cup lemon juice and 1 cup water. Bring to a boil and simmer the breasts, covered, about 20 minutes. In the meantime in another frying pan sauté onions, green pepper, and mushrooms in the butter until some of the liquid from the mushrooms has evaporated, about 5 minutes. Add carrots, cabbage, and squash, and sauté another 2–3 minutes. Add 1 cup of chicken stock to the vegetables with the sour cream and horseradish. Simmer just a minute or so. Then take it off the heat. Preheat oven to 350 degrees. In a shallow roasting pan place a cup of the cooked kasha under each breast. Smother with vegetable smetna sauce and bake about 15 minutes. Serves 6.

🐦 🐟

Try this—just take our word for it—and you'll cook it often in the time to come. It's the kind of recipe you'd never think of making on your own, but it grows on you—and your family.

Chicken Keskeg—Traditional

SERVING TIME: 10–15 MINUTES

1½ cups barley
4½ quarts chicken stock
One 2½–3-pound chicken,
  cut up
2 cloves garlic, minced
Juice of 2 lemons

¼ cup melted butter
Ground cumin (see directions)
Ground chili (see directions)
Yogurt if desired
Fresh mint, chopped, if desired

In a 6–8-quart pot put barley, stock, chicken, garlic, and juice of 1 lemon. Bring to a boil, lower heat, cover, and simmer for 1 hour. Then remove the chicken. Cover the pot and allow to continue simmering while you remove the chicken from the bones. Shred the chicken fine. Add the shredded chicken to the pot and continue cooking the rest of the day. This is a dish which is usually beaten to a mush. You don't have to do that. The flavor is delicious as is, and the extra simmering helps the flavors to blend. When you're ready to serve the keskeg, melt the butter and add about ¼ teaspoon of the cumin and ¼ teaspoon of the chili for each portion. Also add the juice of the second lemon. Mix well and pour a little of this over each serving. Many Middle Easterners like to serve this with dollops of yogurt and fresh chopped mint sprinkled on top. Serves 6.

Try serving this traditional dish with *very* thin tortillas made with whole-wheat flour (chapatis). That's the way the Chinese used to eat this kind of dish many thousands of years ago. You'll understand why.

Chicken with Vegetables, Chinese Style—Traditional

SERVING TIME: 25–35 MINUTES

2 tbsps. oil
2 cloves garlic, minced
2 large onions, chopped
2 bunches green onions, chopped
2 green peppers, chopped
4 raw chicken breasts, boned and sliced (2 to 2½ pounds)
2 cups chopped celery
1 cup carrots, cut in rounds
3 cups bean sprouts

6–8 sliced dried Chinese mushrooms, soaked 15 minutes in warm water
½ cup sliced water chestnuts
½ cup bamboo shoots
1 cup chicken stock
2 tbsps. soy sauce
2 tbsps. molasses
1 tbsp. Chinese sesame oil (optional, but worth getting as a little goes a long way)
1 cup sliced almonds or cashews (optional)

In a large frying pan over high heat stir-fry the garlic, onions, green onions, and green peppers in the oil for about a minute. Add the boned, sliced raw chicken breasts and stir-fry about 5 minutes, until the chicken is cooked. Add the celery, carrots, bean sprouts, mushrooms, water chestnuts and bamboo shoots, stir-frying until everything is well mixed, another 2–3 minutes. Add the stock, soy sauce, molasses, and Chinese sesame oil and nuts if desired. Stir-fry another couple of minutes and serve immediately on homemade noodles (pasta made with eggs), or brown rice. Serves 6.

❀ ❀

This is the chicken version of "chalupas"—with the modifications that adapt it to the different flavor of chicken. We calculate the average person should be able to eat about two of these the *second* time you serve the dish. The first time, make extra, because they taste so good almost everyone overdoes it a bit.

Chicken Chalupas—Traditional

SERVING TIME: 20–30 MINUTES

1 medium head cabbage,
*   finely shredded*
2 green peppers, finely sliced
3 tomatoes, chopped
1 medium onion, finely sliced
4–5 sprigs Chinese parsley
*   (cilantro) **or** 4–5 sprigs reg-*
*   ular parsley, 2 tsps. ground*
*   coriander seeds, 1 tsp.*
*   chervil, and 2 tsps. oregano*
⅓ cup oil

⅓ cup vinegar
1 tsp. freshly ground black
*   pepper, or more, to taste*
3 cups mashed beans (see
*   Frijoles recipe, Chapter 8)*
12 tortillas
One 2½–3 pound chicken,
*   boiled and boned and*
*   chopped or shredded **or***
*   3 cups leftover chicken,*
*   chopped*

In a salad bowl toss the cabbage, green peppers, tomatoes, onion, and the Chinese parsley (cilantro) or the regular parsley with its spices with the oil and vinegar, and black pepper. Heat the mashed beans. Lay out the tortillas. Spread ¼ cup of the mashed beans on each tortilla. On top put about ¼ cup of the chicken. Cover generously with several heaping spoonfuls of salad. Put 2 chalupas on each plate. Serves 6.

❀ ❀

Peking duck is a magnificent recipe that will linger long in the memory of your family and your guests. As usual, most commercial versions are atrocities. Drop into your neighborhood

"Chinese" restaurant and they will serve—usually—hard little squares of unidentifiable and often inedible clinkers soaked in hot grease. Originally, Peking duck only consisted of the skin of the duck, but nowadys, since the meat tastes so good, we think you deserve to have that, too. You can serve it with very thin chapatis—a piece of duck, a section of green onion slightly shorter than the diameter of the chapatis, roll it all up and there you are! Of course, you can use chicken, too, and the recipe should work out equally well with turkey—although, to be honest, we've never tried it that way.

Peking Duck—Traditional

SERVING TIME: 15–20 MINUTES

2 ducks
4–5 cloves garlic, minced
¼ cup finely chopped green
   onions
3 tbsps. soy sauce
3 tbsps. molasses
1 tbsp. cinnamon
¼ tsp. cloves

¼ tsp. aniseed, crushed or
   ground
1 tbsp. wine vinegar
½ tsp. freshly ground black
   pepper
Basting Sauce:
3 tbsps. soy sauce
6 tbsps. honey
2 tbsps. wine vinegar

Put a large kettle of water on to boil. When it is boiling, scald the ducks a few times by dipping them in and out of the boiling water. Drain. In the meantime in a small saucepan put the garlic, green onions, soy sauce, molasses, cinnamon, cloves, aniseed, wine vinegar, and freshly ground black pepper. Cook for a minute or two. Put half of this mixture in each of the ducks and sew the opening closed. Put the ducks on a rack in a roasting pan and paint the basting sauce all over them. Bake in a preheated 500-degree oven for 5 minutes. Baste the ducks again, cover well with aluminum foil, sealing the edges well, and reduce heat to 400 degrees. Roast for another 40–50 minutes. Uncover and baste again and roast, uncovered, until the ducks become nice and crisp, about another 50–60 minutes, turning them from time to time to crisp them all over. Cut the ducks into bite-size pieces with poultry shears. Serve with chapatis (p. 69) or slices of steamed yeast rolls (p. 57) and lots of green onions. Serves 6.

The stuffing here is a main event—not just something to puff out the tomatoes. You'll find that they are very filling—and very satisfying.

Shrimp or Chicken-Stuffed Tomatoes—Traditional

SERVING TIME: 20–30 MINUTES

12 large tomatoes
2 tbsps. olive oil
2 cloves garlic, minced
2 onions, chopped
1 green pepper, chopped
¼ cup chopped parsley
1 tbsp. crushed basil
¼ tsp. crushed fennel seed
1 tsp. freshly ground black
pepper

1½ pounds shelled, chopped
shrimp or 1½ pounds
boned, chopped chicken
breasts
Juice of 1 lemon
½ cup Romano cheese
¼ cup Parmesan cheese
½ cup grated Jack, Muenster
or mozzarella cheese
½ cup bran

Cut the tops off the tomatoes. Save. Scoop out the insides and reserve. In a large frying pan sauté the garlic, onions, green pepper, and parsley in the oil for about a minute. Add tomato pulp, basil, fennel seed, and black pepper. Sauté another minute. Add shrimp or chicken and sauté for five minutes, or until the shrimp or chicken is well cooked, stirring frequently. Add lemon juice, cheeses, and bran. Sauté another minute. Stuff tomatoes, replace tops, and bake in a shallow open baker large enough to accommodate the tomatoes for 20–30 minutes. Serves 6.

Variation:
Stuff large green peppers and use 3 tomatoes, liquefied, in place of tomato pulp in above recipe. Bake for 30–40 minutes.

🐟🐟

Paella is *not* something you whip up after coming home late from a hard day at the office. It is an elegant classic dish that takes time and effort—and amply rewards anyone who makes it and everyone who eats it. Paella has been degraded over the years, until now many restaurant versions are made with frozen vegetables, a few shreds of chicken, and a lot of rice. Do it carefully and lovingly and you'll smile for hours after you eat it.

Paella (High-fiber version)—Traditional

SERVING TIME: 35–45 MINUTES

½ cup chickpeas
½ pound chorizo **or** ½ pound
   ground pork
2 tsps. ground chili
1 clove garlic, mashed
½ tsp. crushed cumin seeds
1 tsp. crushed dried oregano
1 tbsp. vinegar
3 tbsps. olive oil
2 cloves garlic, minced
2 large onions, chopped
One 2½–3 pound chicken, cut
   up in pieces
2 cups washed brown rice

2 tsps. turmeric
4 cups chicken stock
3 tomatoes, chopped
2 green peppers, sliced in
   strips
½ cup fresh green beans, cut
   in thirds
½ cup fresh peas
6 fresh artichoke hearts (cook
   artichokes about 20 minutes
   and take out hearts)
2 cups shredded cabbage
½ pound shelled shrimp
Meat of 1 lobster, cut in chunks

Cook the chickpeas in 3 cups of water in advance for an hour and a half. Drain. Cut up the chorizo in pieces, or mix together in a small bowl the ground pork, spices, and vinegar. In a large frying pan put the olive oil, and over high heat sauté the garlic and onions for a minute or so. Add the cut-up pieces of chicken and brown them. With a slotted spoon remove the browned chicken and onions to a platter. In the remaining oil sauté the washed brown rice until each grain is coated and begins to take on a golden brown. This is best done over a medium to high heat, stirring constantly. Reduce heat to low. Add turmeric and stock and let bubble a few minutes. In the meantime butter or grease a deep 4–5 quart-casserole or dutch oven. Put half of the chicken and onions on the bottom of the casserole. Spread half of the chorizo or pork mixture on top, half the chickpeas, half the tomatoes, half the green peppers, half the green beans, half the peas, half the artichoke hearts and half the cabbage. Pour half the rice broth over all of this, and put the remaining chicken, chorizo or pork mixture, chickpeas, tomatoes, green peppers, green beans, peas, artichoke hearts, and cabbage on top. Pour remaining rice mixture on top and bake, uncovered, for about 40 minutes. Add more stock, if necessary, as paella cooks. Now add the shelled shrimp and lobster and cook another 20 minutes. Traditionally, this dish contains fresh, scrubbed mussels and/or clams in their shells. If you can find fresh, uncontaminated ones, add about a dozen of one or each when you add the shrimp and lobster. Serves 6–8.

🐟🦞

Originally, this was called *langosta enchilada* (lobster in chili-flavored sauce). But the price of lobster meat went through the roof, so the name was changed to protect the consumer. The new name means "seafood in chili-flavored sauce," and the "chili" doesn't mean "hot." You can use any firm fresh fish, even squid or octopus if you feel so inclined. Try to make this a few hours before serving time and refrigerate. Heat just before serving.

Mariscos Enchilados—Traditional

SERVING TIME: 15 MINUTES

2 tbsps. butter **or** oil
3 large onions, chopped
3 cloves garlic, minced
6 large tomatoes, chopped
¼ cup parsley, chopped
3 pounds fish, shelled shrimp,
   or lobster, or any combination of these

1–2 tbsps. ground chili **or**
   ¼–½ cup chopped small
   hot green chilis, 2 tsps. cinnamon, 2 tsps. crushed
   cumin seeds, 2 tsps. crushed
   oregano

In a large frying pan sauté the onions and garlic in the butter or oil until the onions become transparent. Add tomatoes and parsley, and sauté another minute. Add fish or shelled shrimp or lobster, or any combination of same, ground chili or chopped green chilis, cinnamon, cumin, and oregano. Cover and simmer about 10–15 minutes. Serve over brown rice or bulghur. Serves 6–8.

🐟 🦐

The same rules as usual for soy sauce—if you want to use it, fine. The seafood here soaks up the flavor of the sauce as it cooks, and releases it as you savor each tiny tasty morsel. Don't overcook.

Shrimp or Lobster with Vegetables, Chinese Style— Traditional

SERVING TIME: 15 MINUTES

2 tbsps. oil
2 cloves garlic, minced
1–2 tbsps. fresh ginger, minced
2 onions, sliced thin
2 bunches green onions,
  chopped
2 green peppers, sliced
1 cup celery, chopped
1½ pounds shelled shrimp or
  lobster meat

3 cups fresh bean sprouts
½ cup water chestnuts
½ cup bamboo shoots
½ cup chicken stock
2 tbsps. soy sauce
2 tbsps. molasses
1 tbsp. Chinese sesame oil
  (optional, but sensational)

In a large frying pan sauté the garlic, ginger, onions, green onions, and green peppers in the oil about a minute. Add the celery, and sauté another minute or so. Add the shrimp or lobster meat and sauté another 3–4 minutes. Add bean sprouts, water chestnuts, bamboo shoots, chicken stock, soy sauce, molasses, and Chinese sesame oil. Cover and simmer 5 minutes. Serves 6.

🐦 🦐

This is a lovely recipe. Use your own chicken stock, good-quality cheese and fresh shrimp. Unfortunately "fresh" is a relative word when it comes to shrimp. Most shrimp sold in the U.S. are quick-frozen, especially away from the coasts, and can show up as "quick-thawed" in your local supermarket. It pays to ask, but in the meantime never refreeze shrimp—you may be doing it the second or third time. This dish is also very filling—just a little fresh fruit for dessert should be more than enough.

Shrimp-Rice Casserole—Traditional

SERVING TIME: 25–30 MINUTES

2 tbsps. butter **or** oil
3 cloves garlic, minced
2 onions, chopped
½ cup chopped celery
1 carrot, diced
1 bunch green onions,
    chopped
¼ cup chopped parsley
1 green pepper, chopped
1½ pounds shelled shrimp (or
    lobster or crab or combina-
    tion)

2 cups washed brown rice
2 medium tomatoes, liquefied
    in blender (2 cups)
2¼ cups chicken stock
1 tbsp. crushed basil
1 tsp. crushed oregano
Juice of 1 lemon
1 cup Muenster, Jack or
    mozzarella cheese, grated
    (in blender)
½ cup Romano cheese

In a large frying pan sauté the garlic, onions, celery, carrot, green onions, parsley, and green pepper in the butter or oil about 2 minutes. Add the shellfish and sauté another 3–4 minutes. Add brown rice, liquefied tomatoes, stock, basil, oregano, and lemon juice. Mix well. When the broth begins to boil, lower heat, cover, and simmer 35–40 minutes. Now add the cheeses, blend well, cover, and simmer another 5 minutes. Serves 6.

You actually bake the curry into the shrimp—so it really penetrates right to the core. For color and satisfaction, this one is hard to beat.

Curried Shrimp Casserole—Traditional

SERVING TIME: 20 MINUTES

2 tbsps. butter
3 large onions, chopped
1 bunch green onions, chopped
2 green peppers, chopped
1 bunch celery, chopped with leaves

½ pound mushrooms, sliced (optional)
4 large tomatoes, chopped
¼ cup chopped parsley
2–3 tbsps. Madras curry
4 eggs, slightly beaten
2 pounds shelled shrimp

In a large frying pan sauté the onions, green onions, and green peppers in the butter about a minute or so. Add the celery, and sauté another minute. Add the mushrooms, and sauté until some of the water evaporates. Add the tomatoes and sauté another 30 seconds. Take the frying pan off the heat and mix in the parsley, Madras curry, eggs, and shrimp. Pour all this into a greased 3–3½-quart casserole and bake in preheated 350-degree oven about 30 minutes. Serves 6.

This is actually a process of "instant pickling" for a sweet-and-sour fish dish that is beyond compare. It gets better with each passing day—up to six days, but it will never last that long unless you put it in a safe.

Cold Fish Casserole, Russian Style—Traditional

SERVING TIME: 15–20 MINUTES

2 tbsps. olive oil
3 large onions, sliced
1 small cabbage, shredded
3 carrots, cut julienne
6 tomatoes, chopped
¼ cup chopped fresh dill, **or**
   1 tbsp. dry dill weed

¼ cup wine vinegar
½ cup fish or chicken stock
3 tbsps. honey
1 tsp. ground cloves
1 tsp. freshly ground black
   pepper
2 pounds white fish, fillets

In a large frying pan over high heat sauté the onions in the olive oil for a minute or so. Add cabbage and carrots, and sauté another minute. Add tomatoes and dill, and sauté another minute. Add wine vinegar, stock, honey, cloves, and black pepper. Nestle the fish among the vegetables, cover and simmer about 15 minutes, or until you can flake the fish with a fork. Chill. Serve with thick slices of whole-wheat bread. Serves 6.

The wonderful thing about this recipe is that the flavors cook first into the barley and then, as the cooking proceeds, into the fish.

Fish Baked with Vegetable-Barley Stuffing—Traditional

SERVING TIME: 15 MINUTES

3 tbsps. butter
2 large onions, chopped
1 green pepper, chopped
1½ cups chopped celery
½ pound mushrooms, sliced
Juice of 2 lemons
2 cups cooked barley
¼ cup chopped parsley

¼ cup chopped fresh dill
1 tsp. freshly ground black
   pepper
½ cup chopped nuts
3 pounds white fish, fillets (6
   pieces, if possible, of equal
   size)
Additional butter

Preheat oven to 350 degrees. In a medium-size frying pan sauté the onions, green pepper, celery, and mushrooms in the butter until most of the liquid from the mushrooms evaporates. Add the juice of 1 lemon, barley, parsley, dill, black pepper, and nuts. Mix well. Butter a shallow roasting pan and lay half the fillets on the bottom. Spread the vegetable-barley mixture evenly on top of the fillets, and then top with the remaining fillets. Dot the top with butter and squeeze the second lemon over all. Bake for 20–30 minutes, or until the fish flakes. Serve with lemon wedges. Serves 6.

8

Vegetables

America has presided over the death of the vegetable! You don't believe it? Well, let's take a closer look.

How many different kinds of vegetables have you eaten in your life? Fifteen? Twenty? An adventurous *fifty*? There are over two hundred different types of vegetables grown commercially in the United States, and yet the average person has probably been exposed to less than two dozen. Even those vegetables that do fight their way onto the menu arrive in barely recognizable form, since the majority of vegetable eaters consume canned, dried, frozen. and otherwise embalmed produce.

Let's see what happens to a typical canned vegetable—just for fun: Ignoring for the moment the hormones, insecticides, fungicides, and other assorted poisons carefully (and expensively) applied to your future nutrients, your future vegetable course is harvested, dumped in the back of trucks and carted off to the warehouse. Often vegetables are picked long before they ripen and are then preserved and fumigated in warehouses until the most profitable moment for canning arrives. At that moment they may be doped with an artificial ripening chemical to bring them, as they say in those ads, "to the peak of mouth-watering perfection."

The more-or-less ripe vegetables go to a pre-peeling chemical solution of strong alkali to partially dissolve their skins. Then some varieties have to be hardened in another solution to make them firm enough so they don't fall apart in the can. That's the way those nice plump tomatoes get so plump, by the way.

That's just the beginning. The chemical-weary and somewhat wilted vegetables now go to the make-up department, where they are dosed with color-retaining and enhancing chemicals like ethylenediamine tetracetate and sodium metabisulfite, among others. Then a fast shot of monosodium glutamate to try and hype up whatever flavor may accidentally remain, a few more chemicals, a lot of salt, and maybe some sugar to cover up the bitterness of all the gunk that they have soaked up, and into the pressure cooker to have the last vestiges of nutrition bubbled away. If your children won't eat canned peas or canned string beans or canned tomatoes, it's only because they're smarter than you are. Any resemblance between the mish-mash behind those eye-catching labels and a real vegetable would be more than coincidental—it would be a miracle! (Frozen vegetables are a little better, and re-manufactured vegetables like instant mashed potatoes are somewhat worse.)

Actually, vegetables wouldn't deserve so much attention except for the fact that they are one of the most important sources of fiber in the diet. Without a suitable intake of vegetables it is virtually impossible to maintain a high-fiber diet—and overprocessed vegetables cut fiber consumption in two ways. First, they taste so bad no one wants to eat very much of them. Secondly, processing can significantly lower the fiber content of certain vegetables. So, fresh is best.

Don't worry about getting fat on certain vegetables. If you cook them without sugar and don't add excessive amounts of fat, vegetables won't add weight. So you can enjoy beans, potatoes, peas, and other vegetables mislabled "starchy." It has always struck me as slightly tragic to watch a weight-conscious friend pass up a hearty high-fiber potato in order to squeeze a big dish of chemicalized ice cream into his daily calorie quota.

If you possibly can, grow your own vegetables. Nothing compares with a glistening ear of corn, fresh from your corn rows and eaten raw. (Or dropped into already boiling water, if you prefer.) You can grow varieties of vegetables you will never find in your supermarket simply because they do not ship well or keep for weeks on the shelf. Look for special old-fashioned varieties of melons, beets, tomatoes, peas, corn, and carrots.

If you can't grow your own, seek out friends who do, or an enterprising truck farmer or farmer's market. Find out what kinds of poisons your growers apply to your food, and don't hesitate to suggest that they eliminate spraying. Remember that farmers grew enough to feed nations—even in such barren and densely populated countries as Japan—long before DDT was ever invented. You *can* grow crops profitably and successfully without insecticides and pesticides. Smart farmers in the U.S. are doing it every day.

So, adding fresh tasty vegetables to your diet will solve a lot of problems. Your fiber consumption will increase, you should feel better and live longer, and as a fringe benefit maybe you won't have to nag your kids to "Just eat a little bit of vegetable, please?"

Recipes

There is no meat in this dish—and it doesn't suffer at all. Strangely, the mushrooms seem to take up the slack. Be careful not to overcook; remember, you could eat everything here raw and it wouldn't do a bit of harm.

Bean Sprouts and Cabbage, Chinese Style— Traditional

SERVING TIME: 10–15 MINUTES

3 tbsps. butter **or** oil
2 onions, chopped
½ cup chopped green onions
3 cloves garlic
1 medium cabbage, coarsely
   shredded
2 cups fresh bean sprouts
6–8 dried Chinese mushrooms,
   soaked in warm water for
   15 minutes, drained, and
   sliced **or** ¼ pound fresh
   mushrooms, sliced

¼ cup bamboo shoots
¼ cup water chestnuts
3 carrots, cut julienne
2 tbsps. soy sauce
3 tbsps. molasses
1 tbsp. finely chopped ginger,
  or 1 tbsp. ground ginger

In a large frying pan over high heat sauté onions and green onions with garlic in the butter or oil for a minute or so. Add the other vegetables and stir-fry another 2–3 minutes. Add soy sauce, molasses, and ginger, and stir-fry another couple of minutes. (Stir-frying is cooking at high heat, stirring constantly.) Serve immediately. Serves 6.

In Spanish-speaking countries black beans over rice is called *moros y cristianos*—or "Moors and Christians." It's a super high-fiber dish, and you don't have to worry about the calories. With home-cooked beans and brown rice, you can't eat enough to make you fat. The *frijoles refritos* are something wonderful. Black beans are best but other beans are okay, too. The fiber content is right up there where it should be, and you and your family will love the flavor. These mashed beans with a difference are perfect on tortillas, baked crisp tortillas (tostadas), chapatis, or just as a dip. But don't put them on synthetic snack products like imitation potato chips, cheese wuffies, or other junk. Wholesome food screams for more wholesome food. That's another fascinating thing—after a few weeks on a *real food* diet, no one in your family will be able to tolerate those glowing plastic synthetic food master-pieces right off the television screen.

Frijoles—Traditional

SERVING TIME: 5 MINUTES

2 cups pinto, black, or kidney beans
3 large onions, quartered
2 green peppers, quartered

3–4 sprigs of cilantro (Chinese parsley; optional)
3–4 cloves garlic

In a 2½–3-quart saucepan put the beans, onions, green peppers, cilantro, and garlic and cover well with water. Bring to a boil, lower heat, cover and simmer 1½–3 hours, depending on the beans. They should be soft and slightly split. These beans can be served like this or over rice. However, they are also good mashed and fried—*frijoles refritos*. Serves 6.

Frijoles Refritos

SERVING TIME: 10 MINUTES

In a large frying pan put 2 tablespoons of oil. When hot, gradually put in beans, using a slotted spoon to remove them from their broth. Mash the cooked beans with a potato masher. Add 1 tablespoon crushed oregano, 1 tablespoon crushed cumin seeds, and 3 or 4 more sprigs of cilantro, minced. Mash and cook the beans until they pull together into a thick paste without lumps. Serve on tortillas, chapatis, or Mexican rice. Serves 6.

Variation:
Add ½ pound of Jack cheese, Muenster, or cheddar cheese in chunks when frying beans. Cheese will melt and blend into beans.

Quick and Easy (SERVING TIME: 3 MINUTES)
You can also mash the beans in your blender. Even though this takes a bit of the bean broth to accomplish, when you fry the liquefied beans in the oil, as they cook, the excess liquid will evaporate. The extra spices can be added to the blender before frying the beans.

🔥 🔥

Celery and onions each bring something special to the marriage —flavor, texture, and a delicate color. A green pepper is the finishing touch.

Celery-Onion Sauté—Traditional

SERVING TIME: 15–20 MINUTES

3 tbsps. olive oil
2–3 cloves garlic, minced
3 large onions, chopped
2 bunches celery, chopped

1 medium green pepper,
  chopped
½ tsp. sage
½ tsp. marjoram
¼ cup chopped parsley

In a large frying pan put the oil, and when it's hot, sauté the garlic for a minute. Then add the onions, celery, green pepper, and spices, and sauté 2–3 minutes, stirring frequently. Add the parsley, and sauté another minute. Serves 4–6.

🐟 🦀

Half the pleasure of this wonderful dish is its name. In Turkish it means, more or less, "When he tasted this magnificent combination of flavors the prince fainted with delight." If it happens in your family, second helpings are guaranteed to revive the fallen.

Imam Bayaldi—Traditional

SERVING TIME: 15–20 MINUTES

2 medium eggplants
Salt
Olive oil to brush on eggplant
½ cup olive oil
½ large head garlic, minced
3 onions, sliced
2 medium green peppers, chopped

2 large tomatoes, chopped
¼ cup chopped parsley
½ tsp. freshly ground black pepper
2 large tomatoes, liquefied in blender

Wash eggplant well and slice in ¼-inch rounds, leaving on the skin. Place the rounds side by side on a towel and sprinkle them with salt. Let them stand like this for about an hour. Then wash them very thoroughly to remove as much of the salt as possible. Dry well with another clean towel. Place them on a greased baking sheet, brush with olive oil, and roast in a very hot preheated oven, 450 degrees, for about 7 minutes, or until they are light brown. In the meantime in the ½ cup olive oil sauté the garlic, onions, and green peppers at high heat for about 2 minutes. Add the chopped tomatoes, parsley, and black pepper. Sauté everything about 3 minutes more. In a rectangular baking dish (10 x 6 x 2 inches) put half of the eggplant rounds, slightly overlapped if necessary. Pour the stuffing over the slices and top with the rest of the slices. Pour over the liquefied tomatoes and bake 25–30 minutes. Chill. Serve cold. Serves 6.

🪷 🌀

If you like crispy eggplant but you don't want to fry it, this is ideal. The best eggplant to use for this one is the long thin Armenian or Japanese variety, but if you use the salting technique —and carefully wash the salt away after you're through—it will be just as delicious. Use the best Parmesan cheese you can find— pass up the pregrated in those little boxes with the colors of the Italian flag.

Baked Eggplant Slices—Traditional
SERVING TIME: 10 MINUTES

2 *medium eggplants*	2 *tbsps. grated Parmesan*
Salt	*cheese*
2 *eggs, well beaten*	1 *tbsp. crushed oregano*
1 *cup bran*	¼ *tsp. powdered garlic*

Preheat oven to 400 degrees. Wash and slice the eggplants to ¼ inch thickness, leaving the skin on. Lay the slices on a towel, sprinkle with salt, and let them stand for an hour. Prepare two bowls, one with the beaten eggs and one with the bran, cheese, and spices. When the hour is up, wash the eggplant slices very well to remove as much of the salt as possible. Dry well. Then dip the slices into the egg and then into the bran mixture and lay on a greased cookie sheet. Bake about 10 minutes. Turn and bake 3–5 minutes longer. Serves 6.

🪷 🌀

Eggplant is one of the few vegetables that has the same fiber content cooked or raw. This recipe is Armenian, Turkish, Greek, and a lot of other countries. The sesame seeds should be ground to a paste, which adds plenty of fiber. Be sure to get the whole-grain sesames.

Stuffed Eggplants with Sesame-Seed Paste— Traditional

SERVING TIME: 15 MINUTES

3 *small eggplants*
Salt
2 *tbsps. olive oil*
4 *cloves garlic, minced*
2 *medium onions, chopped*

¼ *cup chopped parsley*
Juice of 2–3 lemons to taste
4 *tbsps. tahini* **or** ⅓ *cup*
  sesame seeds, ground in
  blender

Cut the eggplants in half and soak them in salted water for an hour, cut side down. Then wash them well and dry them. Roast them in the oven at 400 degrees for about 20 minutes. When they're soft, remove them from the oven and scoop out the pulp, being careful not to tear the skins. Chop the pulp. In the olive oil sauté the garlic and onions about a minute. Add the eggplant pulp and sauté another minute. Then add parsley, lemon juice, and ground sesame seeds or tahini. Mix well. Fill the skins with the mixture and broil 3 inches below source of heat for 5 minutes. Serves 6.

Variation:
2 *tbsps. olive oil*
2 *medium onions, chopped*
2–3 *cloves garlic, minced*
2 *large tomatoes, chopped*
1 *tbsp. crushed basil*

¼ *cup chopped parsley*
3 *tbsps. Romano or Parmesan*
  cheese
½ *cup grated mozzarella,*
  Muenster, or Jack cheese

Follow the above instructions for eggplant. Sauté onions and garlic in olive oil a minute or two. Add tomatoes and spices. Sauté another minute or two. Add the cheeses. Fill the skins and broil for 5 minutes.

🌶🌶

Leeks are the national emblem of Wales, which gives the Welsh the added distinction of being one of the few national groups to have a high-fiber symbol. (The Scottish thistle does *not* qualify.) Leeks are also mighty good eating and seem to have an affinity for mustard. Try them.

Leeks in Mustard Sauce—Traditional

SERVING TIME: 5 MINUTES

6 leeks
¼ cup olive oil or other salad oil
¼ cup lemon juice **or** *wine vinegar*

1½ tsps. prepared mustard
Freshly ground pepper to taste
Pinch of cayenne pepper

Trim the leeks, cut them in half lengthwise, and wash them well in between each leaf. Bring a large pot of water to boil. Meanwhile, tie the leeks in a bundle and immerse in the boiling water. Let them cook about 5 minutes. In a blender blend the remaining ingredients. Pour over the hot, drained leeks and put into the refrigerator to chill for several hours or overnight. Serves 6.

🌶🌶

Every day over 300 million people eat lentils. Maybe they know something you don't know. Remember to add cumin—it gives those little lentils the zip they need.

Lentils—Traditional

SERVING TIME: 5–7 MINUTES

1½ cups lentils
6 cups water
2 tbsps. olive or salad oil
1 large onion, sliced
1 large green pepper, diced

3 carrots, diced
¼ cup chopped parsley
1 tbsp. cumin
¼ tsp. freshly ground black pepper

In a 2½–3-quart saucepan put the lentils and water. Bring to a boil, cover and simmer about 20 minutes. In a frying pan put the oil and when hot, sauté the onion, green pepper, and carrots about 2 minutes. Add the parsley, sauté a few seconds more, and mix in with the lentils and spices. Cook the lentils, covered, another 15 minutes. Serves 6.

🔥 🔥

Few Americans eat lentils this way, probably because they don't know the recipe exists. It is one of the most sensational vegetable plates we have come across—even after enjoying it for fourteen years or so, we still come back for more. Use freshly squeezed lemon juice, by all means. That junk in the bottles has no place in your kitchen.

Lentil Platter—Traditional

SERVING TIME: 10 MINUTES

1 tbsp. butter or oil
2–3 cloves garlic, minced
1 cup lentils
2½ cups water
¼–½ tsp. freshly ground
  black pepper

⅓ cup cracked wheat
3 large onions, minced
½ cup minced parsley
Juice of 3 lemons or more to
  taste

In a 1½–2-quart saucepan melt the butter or oil and sauté the garlic for a minute or so. Add the lentils, water, and black pepper, and bring to a boil. Then lower heat and simmer, covered, about 45 minutes. Add cracked wheat to lentils, cover, and simmer another 5 minutes. Spread lentils on a platter and chill. Serve cold, smothered with minced onions, parsley, and lots of lemon juice. Serves 6.

🔥🔥

If you use an okra pod over 3 inches long, we decline all responsibility for the success of this formulation. Up to 2 and 99/100 inches, okra is tender, delicate, delightful. Over 3 inches, it can be tough and ill-mannered. A lot of people like this dish cold the next day—you might be one of them.

Okra Casserole—Traditional

SERVING TIME: 10–15 MINUTES

2 tbsps. olive oil
2 cloves garlic, minced
2 medium onions, sliced
2 medium green peppers, sliced
4 large tomatoes, chopped
1 tsp. crushed oregano

Freshly ground black pepper to taste
⅛ tsp. crushed hot peppers or more to taste **or** several drops Tabasco to taste
Juice of 1 lemon
2 pounds okra

In a large frying pan sauté the garlic, onions, and green peppers in the oil for a minute or so. Add the tomatoes, oregano, black pepper, hot peppers or tabasco, and lemon juice. Sauté another minute. Correct seasoning. Add the okra. Mix the ingredients, cover, and simmer about 15 minutes. This can be served hot or cold. Serves 6.

🔥🔥

This dish is even more sensational if it has been prepared a day or so in advance. Ratatouille has pleased the palates of discriminating Frenchmen (and women) for over a thousand years. Use fresh, young vegetables and you can't fail.

Ratatouille, High-Fiber Version— Traditional

SERVING TIME: 20 MINUTES

1 medium eggplant, sliced
3 small zucchini, thinly
    sliced
3 medium onions, sliced
4 medium green peppers,
    sliced

6 fresh artichoke hearts (if
    available)
3 large tomatoes, sliced
4 carrots, sliced on an angle
¼ cup olive oil
3–4 cloves garlic, minced
2 tsps. crushed oregano

Lay the eggplant slices on a clean towel and sprinkle them with a little salt. Let stand 30 minutes to 1 hour. In the meantime prepare the other vegetables. Then wash and dry the eggplant well to remove the excess salt. In a 5-quart dutch oven or a casserole which can be used on top of the stove put the olive oil, garlic, and 1 teaspoon of oregano, and sauté about a minute. Layer the vegetables, putting some of each one in each layer. Sprinkle a little more olive oil on top of the vegetables, about 1 tablespoon, and 1 teaspoon more of oregano, and cover, and cook at medium heat for about 30–40 minutes, gently mixing the vegetables once during the cooking time. Chill. Serve cold, with lemon if desired. Serves 6.

🐚🐚

Compared to this recipe, all other stuffed tomato and pepper recipes are weaklings. Standing shoulder to shoulder with the high fiber are the bold spices. Waiting in reserve are a battalion of variations to make this the recipe for all occasions. *Note.* You can fill zucchini, squash, and cucumbers in the same way—using the pulp for filling. You won't need quite as much water in the roasting pan.

Stuffed Tomatoes and Green Peppers—Traditional

SERVING TIME: 10 MINUTES

6 *large tomatoes*
6 *large green peppers*
3 *medium onions, chopped*
½ *cup washed brown rice*
¼ *cup chopped fresh parsley*

½ *tsp. freshly ground black*
  pepper
1 *tsp. crushed dried oregano*
3–4 *drops Tabasco sauce to*
  taste
2 *cups water*

Wash tomatoes and green peppers well. Cut the tops off, reserving them for later. Scoop out the centers, saving the tomato pulp for the filling. In a bowl put tomato pulp, onions, raw brown rice, parsley, black pepper, oregano, and Tabasco sauce. Mix well. Fill the hollows of the tomatoes and green peppers about two-thirds full. Put 2 tablespoons water into each shell. Replace tops of vegetables. Arrange these side by side in a shallow roasting pan. Add water, cover, and bake in preheated 350-degree oven for 45 minutes to 1 hour. Serves 6.

Variations:
• Add ¼ cup Parmesan cheese to above mixture, and the liquid of two tomatoes, liquefied in blender, divided among the 12 vegetable shells.
• Substitute ¼ cup uncooked barley for the rice; substitute 1 teaspoon crushed dried mint for the oregano; add 2 teaspoons lemon juice to each filled vegetable shell. Proceed as above.
• Substitute ¼ cup cracked wheat for rice; add ¼ cup raisins; ¼ cup nuts, chopped; substitute 1 teaspoon allspice for oregano; add ½ teaspoon cinnamon.
• Substitute ¼ cup buckwheat groats, whole or split, for rice; substitute 2 teaspoons dill for oregano; add 2 teaspoons lemon juice to each filled shell. Serve topped with yogurt if desired.

Quick and Easy
Use about 2 cups leftover cooked rice, cracked wheat, or buckwheat as the cooked grain, proceeding as above in preferred variation.

🌿 🍂

Try to find the smallest squash you can—small means young and tender. Be sure that the raisins don't have anything else written on the box except "raisins"—"moisturizing," preservatives, and stuff like that will not improve your health or the flavor of the recipe. It does improve profits—and hurts your body.

Summer Squash with Raisins and Nuts—Traditional

SERVING TIME: 10 MINUTES

2 tbsps. butter
3 onions, chopped
10–12 small yellow crookneck
   or pattypan squash (about 3
   pounds), medium diced
½ cup raisins

½ cup chopped or slivered
   nuts (almonds go well)
2 tsps. allspice
1 tsp. cinnamon
1 tbsp. honey **or** molasses

In a medium frying pan sauté the onions in the butter until transparent. Add the squash and sauté another couple of minutes. Add raisins, nuts, spices, and honey or molasses. Sauté another minute or so to blend. Simmer 3–5 minutes. Serves 6.

🌿 🍂

Swiss chard is very nice. If you have a square foot or so of soil, you can grow enough for four people. Just pick the outer leaves as they mature and keep the plant from freezing. You can grow it indoors in a container as well. Fresh, crisp, and fibrous—and, if you grow it at home, *free.*

Swiss Chard—Traditional

SERVING TIME: 5 MINUTES

2 tbsps. olive oil
2 cloves garlic, minced
3 pounds Swiss chard,
   chopped

2 medium onions, sliced
Juice of 1 lemon

In a frying pan put the oil and sauté the garlic a minute or so at
high heat. Then add the chard and the onions, sauté a minute or
so. Cover and cook at medium heat about 5 minutes. Serve
sprinkled with lemon juice. Serves 6.

❀ ❀

Simple, elegant, designed to draw out the subtle individual
flavors of each vegetable. We can't say much more than that.
You'll like it.

Baked Mixed Vegetables—Traditional

SERVING TIME: 20–30 MINUTES

1 pound tender asparagus
1 medium cauliflower
1 small bunch broccoli
2 tomatoes
2 medium onions, sliced
½ pound young okra
2 medium yellow squash or
   zucchini, with skin

3–4 eggs, beaten
2 cups bran tossed with 1 tbsp.
   ground marjoram or 1 tbsp.
   ground basil, ¼ cup finely
   chopped parsley, and ½ tsp.
   freshly ground black pepper

Wash and trim the asparagus, leaving only the tenderest part.
Place in a shallow pan and cover with boiling water until you
finish preparing the other vegetables. Then proceed to prepare
the cauliflower and other vegetables. Wash and break the cauliflower into small flowerets. Wash and trim the broccoli, leaving

only the tenderest parts. Cut into bite-size pieces. (You can save the less tender parts of the vegetables to flavor soups with.) Slice the tomatoes and onions in about ¼-inch slices. Wash okra. Wash and slice squash. Drain asparagus. On a greased cookie sheet or two place vegetables, first dipped into the beaten egg and then covered with the bran-spice-parsley mixture. Bake at preheated 375 degrees about 15 minutes. Serves 6–8.

🐚🦀

When your family insists on something "right away"—or you just feel like a high-fiber fix without waiting around—this is one way to do it. Hot, tasty, served with toasted homemade whole-wheat bread and butter—make sure you have enough for seconds!

Gourmet Short-Order Vegetable Fry—Traditional

SERVING TIME: 15–20 MINUTES

1 small cabbage	¼ cup olive or salad oil
3 small zucchini or yellow crookneck squash	2–3 cloves garlic, peeled and minced
2 large tomatoes	Freshly ground black pepper
2 medium onions	1 tbsp. Madras curry powder

Thinly slice the cabbage. Chop the squash and tomatoes. Slice the onions in rounds, and then once in half for half rounds. In a frying pan put the oil. When it gets hot, put in the garlic and onions, and sauté them for a minute or so. Then add the squash and sauté them a minute or so. Then add the coleslaw and sauté it a few minutes, stirring until it wilts a bit. Add tomatoes, ground black pepper, and curry powder. Stir to mix and sauté a couple of minutes more or until vegetables are done to taste. Serves 6.

9
Eggs & Cheese

My, how things do change! Back in 1941 the newspapers were full of stories about the poor under-nourished British children who had to struggle along on *one egg a week!* Now, in the United States, millions of executives (and others who should know better) are piously putting themselves on the desperation diet of Britain's beleaguered waifs.

For at least the past fifteen years in the U.S. there has been a cheese-butter-and-egg phobia—as if the path to perpetual youthfulness made a wide detour around dairy products. I remember my professor of Pathology back in medical school always used to say, "There's no fool like an educated fool!" And then he'd smile and add: "Except, of course, for the half-educated fool . . ."

In a bizarre kind of mania that will ultimately take its place in history with other lesser delusions like the Dutch Tulip Mania and the Florida Land Boom, Americans have been deserting wholesome foods like cheese, butter, and eggs, and gorging on trash barely fit for human consumption. This is the way it happened. Back in the nineteen-thirties clever scientists gave rabbits cholesterol deposits in their little arteries by feeding them a diet that no rabbit in the history of the world ate on his own. The next step was to transfer these interesting—but not exciting—findings to human beings. The word went out—via popularized and somewhat garbled versions—that if you eat the diet of an experimental rabbit, you'll get a heart attack. Amazingly no one ever thought of promoting the opposite. If you stick to the diet of a normal rabbit—let your ears grow, and live in the briar patch—you'll be heart-attack proof. And probably have the life-expectancy of a cottontail as well.

As we have already seen, the food processors—who are in

business to sell their compounds, not necessarily to save lives—capitalized on the fear and anxiety of the population in general. They produced over a thousand products which are guaranteed to be "low in saturated fats," "high in unsaturated and polyunsaturated fats"—and other basically unintelligible gibberish. (Truthfully, not one person in a thousand can define unsaturated fat. "Unsaturated" refers to an organic chemical compound which has double or triple bonds between its carbon atoms.) Even the FDA and the FTC, who usually don't pay much attention to what the food monopolies claim in their advertising, have taken a surprisingly firm stand in this case. Probably because the swindle is so obvious it offends the basically intelligent administrators. *Food processors are absolutely forbidden to claim that any "low-fat," "polyunsaturated" or similar product will have any effect on lowering blood cholesterol.* However, they deliver their message by innuendo, as usual. A full-page ad for "polyunsaturated" mayonnaise inviting you to "ask your doctor" whether it should be "part of your diet" sneaks the message across.

Several brands of margarine are heavily promoted in medical journals with heavy-handed copy like: "Don't your patients deserve the protection of polyunsaturated SMEARY brand margarine?" That kind of dirty pool is routine in the food advertising business—fear and anxiety used to sell texturized and emulsified chemicals as food.

To prove the ultimate absurdity of the hysterical distortion of the American diet, there is a scientific fact that has been ignored by the food processors (of course), by the scientific community (hard to understand), and has been played down in the popular press (so as not to offend advertisers?).

The campaign to eliminate dairy products from the American diet has been in full swing for about fifteen years. During that period of time, the menu of the average American family has been flooded with high-priced substitutes for basic, healthful, inexpensive foods. At the end of 1975 it reached the ultimate absurdity when a Federal Trade Commission administrative "judge" ruled that *cholesterol was not necessary for normal bodily functions!** That ultimate conceit is the equivalent of the American

* *The Wall Street Journal*, December 12, 1975, p. 26, lines 18–20.

Medical Association trying to repeal the Law of Gravity. Since 1960, the level of supposedly hazardous "saturated fats" in the American diet steadily decreased, and the intake of supposedly "protective" "polyunsaturated" fats has steadily increased without reducing the incidence of heart attacks.

To make the situation even more idiotic, most Americans who have renounced eggs and cheese and milk are consuming significant amounts of "saturated" fats without being aware of it. Every commercial food product—candy, cakes, cookies, potato chips, frozen fried foods (onion rings, fish, shrimp, French-fried potatoes), desserts, imitation whipped cream and other "whips," salad dressings, and even boxed breakfast cereals contain coconut oil (or palm-kernel oil) as their sole cooking fat.

These oils are far more hazardous than any other oil or fat in common use—from the standpoint of the "cholesterol theory." In fact, it is much less dangerous, according to the proponents of the theory, to use butter, and even lard, in the human diet than the cheap coconut oil that occupies first place on the American menu. Virtually all fast foods and the majority of candy sold in the United States are prepared with almost totally saturated coconut oil.

With these facts in mind, it makes even more sense to enjoy the nutritional and gourmet value of eggs and cheese in the daily diet, provided you take two precautions: first, maintain a high level of fiber in your daily food intake, and secondly, eliminate the cheap and inferior product that goes under the innocent name of "vegetable oil."

With that out of the way, let's get down to the pleasant task of integrating fresh, wholesome eggs and delicious cheese into the high-fiber diet.

Recipes

Quiche, in a certain way, is the French version of pizza. If you think of it in those terms, you will come up with some great toppings and variations on your own. The choice of white pepper is purely decorative—black pepper is just as good, and even contains a trace more fiber than the white variety. (Black pepper has the outer coat of the pepper included in the grind—white is just the center berry.) Just as in the fondue recipes, use the best cheese you can find. Avoid anything that says "processed cheese," "cheese food," "Swiss-*style*," and other weasel-words.

High-Fiber Quiche—Traditional

SERVING TIME: 15–20 MINUTES

Pastry for a 9-inch shell (see Chapter 5)
½ *cup chopped onions*
½ *cup chopped green pepper*
½ *cup shredded cabbage (This can be done in the blender: put in some of the cabbage, cover with water, blend for just a second, and drain.)*

½ *cup chopped zucchini or yellow squash*
1 *cup grated Swiss cheese (preferably Emmenthal)*
4 *eggs, lightly beaten*
2 *cups half and half*
¼ *tsp. nutmeg*
¼ *tsp. ground white pepper*
¼ *tsp. cayenne pepper*

Line a 9-inch pie plate with pastry. Toss the vegetables with the grated cheese and spread over the pie shell. Beat the eggs with half and half and spices, and pour over the vegetables and cheese. Bake in a preheated 400-degree oven for 10 minutes, and then lower temperature to 350 degrees, and bake 20–30 minutes, until the custard is set and the top becomes a golden brown. Serves 6.

Variations:
• In place of squash, use chopped tomatoes and the following spices: 1 teaspoon crushed oregano, ¼ teaspoon crushed fennel seed, 1 teaspoon crushed basil, ½ teaspoon ground black pepper. Instead of the Swiss cheese use ½ cup grated mozzarella, ½ cup provolone, and ¼ cup Romano. Proceed as above.
• Follow the original recipe, replacing only the cabbage and squash with 1 cup of asparagus tips. Arrange them on the pie crust and proceed as above, tossing the remaining vegetables with the cheese and eggs.
• Substitute cauliflower, broccoli, turnips, or artichoke hearts,

leaving out the cabbage and squash, but using the same proportions—1 cup.

• Mix and match your own favorite combinations. Vegetable combinations, shrimp with mushrooms and onions, cooked ground pork with onions and bean sprouts, and if you want a Chinese flavor replace above spices in the original with ¼ teaspoon black pepper, 1 teaspoon soy sauce, 2 teaspoons molasses, and 1 teaspoon ground ginger or 1 tablespoon fresh ginger, minced.

• Don't be afraid to use leftover vegetables and meats or poultry or fish, vary the spices, and create a masterpiece.

Quick and Easy (SERVING TIME: 5 MINUTES)
If you know that you'll be in a hurry, prepare all the ingredients, except the eggs, in advance and keep in a covered container in the refrigerator. The last-minute putting together will be a cinch.

Super-Instant (SERVING TIME: HALF A MINUTE)
These quiches can be prepared, cooked, and frozen. Then all it takes is a few minutes in a preheated 350-degree oven to warm them up. While you're doing something else.

It would be hard to think of a healthier meal than this one. Crisp fresh vegetables dipped in spicy melted cheese. There are two essential points: first, buy the very best quality cheese you can find. Dipping in second-quality cheese is like dipping in hot paraffin. Secondly, keep the temperature just high enough to keep the cheese liquid—you don't want to cook it.

Vegetable-Cheese Fondue—Traditional

SERVING TIME: 15–20 MINUTES

12 fresh artichoke hearts
½ pound broccoli, broken into flowerets
½ pound asparagus tips
1 cauliflower, broken into flowerets
2 zucchini or yellow squash, cut into bite-size chunks
3 large carrots, cut in rounds
3 raw turnips, cut into bite-size cubes

Chunks of toasted whole-wheat bread
2 tbsps. butter
1 clove garlic, minced
1 pound grated Swiss Emmenthal cheese
3 tbsps. whole-wheat stone-ground or pastry flour
1½ cups half and half
6 egg yolks
¼ tsp. nutmeg
¼ tsp. black pepper

Prepare vegetables. In a large pot of boiling water cook artichokes about 20 minutes. Also cook broccoli and asparagus tips in boiling water about 5 minutes. Do not cook other vegetables. Arrange the vegetables on a large platter. Fill a bowl with chunks of toasted whole-wheat bread.

In a chafing dish over low heat melt the butter and stir garlic around a bit to heat it. Then add the grated cheese and let the cheese melt. It should become creamy. Mix the flour with a small portion of the half and half, then pour the cream and the flour mixture into the chafing dish, and mix well. Gradually beat in the egg yolks, nutmeg, and black pepper. This mixture will thicken a bit.

The platter of vegetables and the chunks of bread can be set on the table, and each person can help himself to a variety— dipping them into the fondue.

🌀🌀

The rules for quesadillas are as fluid as the melted cheese. Almost any kind of pure cheese will do fine, and you can use green onions, white onions, fresh green chilis, and nearly any other taste combination that appeals to you. Never let anyone tel you: "That's the *wrong* way to make that!" When it comes to proportions and variations, we always feel that the right way is the way you feel like doing it. So press on!

Quesadillas—Traditional

SERVING TIME: 10 MINUTES

12 corn tortillas (see Chapter 5)
2 medium onions, chopped
  fine
2 medium tomatoes, chopped
  fine
½ tsp. ground chili

½ tsp. crushed cumin seeds
1 tsp. crushed dried oregano
12 slices of cheddar, mozzarella, Muenster, or Jack
  cheese

On a cookie sheet lay out the tortillas. Prepare the onions and tomatoes, mixing them in a bowl with the spices. Place a tablespoonful or two on each tortilla. On top place a slice of the cheese of your choice. Put under the broiler about 3 inches from source of heat and broil until the cheese is lightly browned. Serves 6.

Quick and Easy (SERVING TIME: 5 MINUTES)
With a push of a button, you can blend the onions, tomatoes, and spices in the blender in seconds. Then proceed as above.

Super-Instant (SERVING TIME: 2 MINUTES)
If you make these up the night before or even a few days before, with a couple of minutes under the broiler, they'll be ready to satisfy.

🔥🔥

In the old Southwest this was a favorite of the *other* cowboys—the Mexican *vaqueros* who rode south of the Rio Grande—or, as they called it, the Rio Bravo. Like all classical dishes, this one shows an instinctive feel for the happy marriage of certain ingredients. The tomato, the egg, and the onion all mingle delightfully, aided by oregano and abetted by ground chili. This is breakfast, lunch, or supper—and a delight every time.

Huevos Rancheros—Traditional

SERVING TIME: 25–30 MINUTES

4 tbsps. butter **or** olive oil
1 clove garlic, minced
2 large onions, chopped
2 large green peppers, chopped
6 large tomatoes, chopped

1 tbsp. crushed oregano
2 tsps. crushed cumin seeds
1 tsp. ground chili
12 eggs
2 tbsps. butter

In a large frying pan sauté the garlic, onions, and green peppers in the butter or oil until the onions become transparent, about a minute or two. Add the tomatoes, oregano, cumin, and chili, and cook about 5 minutes. While the sauce is cooking, break the eggs into a bowl and mix gently with a fork, enough to blend whites and yolks. In another frying pan large enough for the 12 eggs, melt the 2 tablespoons of butter over medium heat. Pour in the eggs. As the eggs begin to cook at the sides of the pan, pull the cooked part into the center and gently scramble the cooked parts of the eggs with the liquid until the eggs are cooked, but moist. Serve the eggs smothered with the sauce, and tortillas or chapatis on the side. Serves 6.

Variation:
Puff omelette—separate the whites from the yolks. Beat the whites separately until they hold stiff peaks. Beat the yolks. Fold the yolks into the whites carefully and pour into frying pan. Lift the edges of the omelette, allowing the liquid to run under. Continue lifting the edges and letting the liquid take the place of the already cooked egg, until there is no more liquid. Cover half of the omelette with filling. Gently tip the pan away from you, folding half of the omelette over the half nearest you. Slide onto plate and pour more of the filling over the top. Cut in wedges and serve. These puff omelettes can be made into 6 individual ones.

Quick and Easy (SERVING TIME: 10 MINUTES)
Put the garlic, onions, green peppers, and tomatoes into the
blender along with the oregano, cumin, and chili. In seconds
you're ready to sauté this mixture in the butter or olive oil and
proceed as above.

Super-Instant (SERVING TIME: 5–7 MINUTES)
This is the kind of sauce that can be made up in advance and
used for quesadillas or small pizzas—using English muffins as the
base—as well as for Huevos Rancheros. If you're ahead of yourself, this scrumptious dish will be ready in no time.

🐾 🐾

Mexicans who go to Spain and order tortillas are shocked when
the waiter brings a big delicious egg omelette. Spaniards who order
a tortilla in Mexico are indignant when the waiter brings them
little corn cakes. But that doesn't bother us, because we know
what to expect from Spanish tortillas—mouthfuls of goodness.

Egg Tortilla—Traditional
SERVING TIME: 15 MINUTES

4 *tbsps. butter* **or** *oil*
1 *large onion, chopped*
1 *large green pepper, chopped*
1 *large potato, washed and*
   diced
1 *carrot, diced*
¼ *pound Spanish sausage—*
   chorizo—sliced (If it's not
   made with nitrates or nitrites

   —or try making the home-
   made kind in Chapter 6.) **or**
   ¼ *pound ground pork sea-*
   soned with ⅛ tsp. crushed
   hot peppers, ½ tsp. crushed
   cumin seeds and ¼ tsp.
   oregano
8 *eggs*

In a large, heavy frying pan sauté the onion and green pepper
in the butter or oil for about a minute. Add the potato and carrot,
and sauté another few minutes, or until the potato begins to fry to
golden brown. In the meantime in a small, heavy frying pan fry

the sausage or pork with spices until well cooked. With a slotted spoon drain the meat and add to the onion-potato mixture. In a large bowl beat the eggs with a fork to mix the whites and yolks well. Pour the eggs over the onion-potato-meat mixture in the pan. The heat should be medium. Lift the sides of the egg tortilla as it is cooking, allowing the liquid to pass to the bottom of the pan. When the egg tortilla seems fairly well cooked, about 5–7 minutes, loosen edges of egg from pan, put a plate over pan, and turn the egg tortilla, and then slide it back into the frying pan to cook another 4–5 minutes. Serves 4–6.

🐟 🐟

Presenting the world's first "Invincible Soufflé"! It will hold its own against a hurricaine, an earthquake, or shaky hands after a hard day with the kids (or the clients). The ingredients aren't too bad either. Cumin seeds give it a unique flavor.

Corn-Onion Soufflé—Traditional

SERVING TIME: 10–15 MINUTES

2¼ cups milk
½ cup and plus 2 tbsps.
    additional cornmeal
6 tbsps. butter
1 tbsp. butter for sautéeing
½ cup chopped onion
½ cup chopped green pepper

2 tbsps. minced hot green
    chili (or substitute ¼ tsp.
    cayenne pepper)
¼ tsp. black pepper
⅛ tsp. nutmeg
½ tsp. crushed cumin seeds
5 eggs, separated

Scald the milk. Add the cornmeal and the 6 tablespoons of butter and beat well, cooking until mixture thickens. In a frying pan sauté the onion and green pepper in the tablespoon of butter. If you use minced hot green chili, sauté it with the onion and green pepper at the same time. If you use the cayene pepper, add it after you sauté the vegetables, along with the black pepper, nutmeg, and cumin. Mix well. Add the vegetable-spice mixture to the cornmeal-milk. Gradually add the egg yolks, beating constantly. In another bowl beat the egg whites until they hold a peak. Beat a couple of spoonfuls of the beaten whites into the corn- meal mixture. Then carefully fold in the rest of the whites. Pour into a well-buttered 2–2½-quart soufflé dish and bake immediately in preheated 350-degree oven for 25 minutes. Serves 4.

Quick and Easy Invincible Soufflés (SERVING TIME: 5–10 MINUTES) Following the above recipe, in a blender put scalded milk, 6 tablespoons butter, cornmeal, hot green chili or cayenne pepper, black pepper, nutmeg, crushed cumin seeds, and eggs (do not separate) and blend for a minute or so. Add the minced onion and green pepper which has been sautéed in the 1 tablespoon butter. Mix with a spoon and pour into a well-buttered 2–2½- quart soufflé dish. Bake in preheated 325-degree oven, set in a deep pan of water, 20–25 minutes, or until firm.

🦅🦅

A wonderful main course, snack, side dish—or whatever excuse you need for eating it any time of the day or night. It's also good —cut into little pieces—for hors d'ouevres, and it's just as good cold as hot.

Frittata—Traditional

SERVING TIME: 10–15 MINUTES

3 tbsps. olive oil
1 clove garlic, minced
1 large onion, thinly sliced
1 large green pepper, thinly
   sliced
2 zuchini, thinly sliced
1 carrot, cut julienne

8 eggs, beaten
¼ cup Parmesan cheese
½ tsp. crushed dried oregano
¼ tsp. freshly ground black
   pepper
½ tsp. basil
¼ tsp. crushed fennel seed

In a frying pan large enough to accommodate the 8 eggs (8–10 inches) heat the oil and sauté the garlic, onion, and green pepper for a minute or so. Add the zucchini and carrot, and sauté for another minute. In a large bowl beat the eggs with the cheese, oregano, black pepper, basil, and fennel seed. Pour the eggs over the vegetables and cook at medium heat, lifting the sides to allow the liquid to run under the frittata. Cook about 5 minutes. Cover the frying pan with a plate and turn the frittata. Slide it back into the frying pan again to cook the other side—about 5 minutes more. Cut into wedges and serve. Serves 6.

Variation:
In place of zucchini, try broccoli, eggplant, other kinds of squash, cabbage, turnips, etc.

Quick and Easy (SERVING TIME: 7–10 MINUTES)
It is easy to prepare these fresh vegetables ahead of time. In a matter of seconds you'll be ready to put the frittata together when you want it.

The usual Chinese restaurant version of Egg Foo Yong is an economy measure—for them. All the leftover vegetables—and goodness knows what else—are dumped into cooked eggs.

That hardly does justice to a noble dish. There are few recipes so simple and pure as Chinese vegetables and fresh eggs. The oyster sauce is a revelation—it seems to clarify the flavors and help them blend. Even using the finest of ingredients, a super meal for six should run about 30 cents a person, more or less. Of course, that's built into the high-fiber way of eating—good food, good flavor, and better health, all for less money than the ugly, dangerous "modern way."

Egg Foo Yong—Traditional

SERVING TIME: 10–15 MINUTES

6 eggs
1 tsp. soy sauce
2 cups fresh bean sprouts
½ cup chopped green onions
½ cup bamboo shoots
½ cup water chestnuts
4 tbsps. butter **or** oil

Sauce:
1 cup chicken stock
1 tbsp. cornstarch
2 tsps. molasses
1 tsp. soy sauce
or
⅔ cup water
4 tbsps. oyster sauce

Beat the eggs in a large mixing bowl with 1 tablespoon soy sauce. Add the vegetables and mix well. In an 8–10-inch frying pan heat the butter or oil until fairly hot, and pour in the egg mixture. Cook on medium heat, allowing the liquid to run underneath by lifting the omelette in different places several times during the 4–5 minutes it takes to cook on one side. Then loosen the omelette from bottom and sides of pan. Cover the frying pan with a large plate and carefully turn the Egg Foo Yong over and onto the plate. Slide the Egg Foo Yong back into the frying pan to cook on the other side about 4–5 minutes, or cook under broiler heat until egg is set. In the meantime heat the stock or water in a saucepan. Mix the cornstarch with a tiny bit of water to make a thickish paste and add to the saucepan, along with either the molasses and soy sauce or the oyster sauce. (They're both good.) Pour this over the Egg Foo Yong and serve cut in wedges. Serves 4.

Variation:
Allow 1 cup cooked beef, chicken, pork, fish, or shellfish, or ½ pound fresh-ground pork to fry up in the oil before you pour in the egg-vegetable mixture.

🌀🌀

This is a fast, sensational little recipe. Be sure to use the fennel seeds—they make a big difference. Grind the pepper fresh each time—any kind of inexpensive pepper grinder will do. But remember that the flavor of pepper is due to the essential oils within the peppercorn. Preground pepper—which can lie in warehouses for months, if not years—has lost much of the oil essence through evaporation.

Egg-Vegetable Casserole—Traditional

SERVING TIME: 20–25 MINUTES

1 cup chopped tomatoes
2 cups shredded cabbage
½ cup diced carrots
½ cup chopped parsley
1 cup chopped leeks
½ cup chopped green peppers
1 cup chopped green beans
½ cup chopped mustard
　greens

½ cup chopped green onions
¼–½ tsp. freshly ground
　pepper to taste
1 tsp. oregano
¼ cup Parmesan cheese
¼ cup Romano cheese
¼ tsp. crushed fennel seed
10 eggs, beaten
4 tbsps. butter

Preheat oven to 350 degrees. In a large bowl toss the prepared vegetables together with the black pepper, oregano, cheeses, and fennel seed. Beat the eggs in a separate bowl, and mix in with the vegetables. Melt the butter in a large 3–3½-quart casserole. Pour the vegetable-egg mixture into the casserole. Top with a little more of either cheese. Bake for 40 minutes, or until top is a golden brown. Serves 6.

How to pick a fresh egg? The best way is to crack the shell and look at the yolk. If it sits up firm and proud, making a half-circle, it's fresh. If it lies there quivering and ashamed, it's probably spent most of its life in cold storage—up to a year or more. If you get flat, watery eggs you need to find a different set of hens to lay for you. Try a ride out in the country to find a farmer who has just a few chickens that run around the yard. The eggs are likely to fertilized, fresh, and uncontaminated. Second-best is a commercial egg ranch, where the eggs will be fresh, period. If you're lucky enough you may have a little space to raise your own chickens. They live on table scraps, a little feed, and can lay up to 350 eggs a year. And what sensational eggs!

Casserole Poached Eggs—Traditional

SERVING TIME: 15–20 MINUTES

4 tbsps. butter
½ cup sliced onions
½ cup thinly sliced green
  peppers
½ cup potatoes, cut julienne
½ cup sliced fresh mushrooms
1 tbsp. parsley
½ cup freshly grated corn
2½ cups chopped tomatoes

1 cup liquefied tomatoes
1 cup beef or chicken stock
½ tsp. tarragon
¼ tsp. chervil
1 tsp. chives
¼ tsp. freshly ground black
  pepper
6 eggs
Paprika or cayenne pepper

In a 2½–3-quart casserole or skillet melt the butter and sauté the onions, green peppers, and potatoes for a minute or so. Add the mushrooms and parsley, and sauté another minute or two. Add the corn, tomatoes, liquefied tomatoes, stock, tarragon, chervil, chives, and black pepper. Cover and simmer about 10 minutes. Uncover and break the eggs into the casserole carefully, spacing 5 around the edge and 1 in the middle. Let the eggs poach in the liquid for 5–6 minutes. When they are cooked, sprinkle the eggs with a little paprika or cayenne pepper and serve. Serves 6.

🌀🌀

What makes these high-fiber egg nests different is the whole-wheat English muffins, the gleaming bright-red tomatoes, and the mellow, nutty Swiss cheese. What a way to start the day, finish the day—or just plain sit down and eat.

Nest of Yolks—Traditional

SERVING TIME: 10 MINUTES

6 whole-wheat English muffins
Butter
12 thin slices of sweet onions
12 thick slices of tomatoes

1½ tsps. tarragon or basil
12 thin slices of Swiss cheese
12 eggs, separated, leaving
   each yolk in half a shell

Preheat oven to 350 degrees. Split the English muffins, butter them, and lay them on a cookie sheet, not too close together. On top of each one lay first a slice of onion, then a slice of tomato, sprinkle with ¼ teaspoon of the tarragon or basil, and add a slice of cheese. In a deep bowl beat the whites of the eggs until they are stiff and hold a peak. Place some on top of each muffin and make a well in the white. Slip the yolk into the well, place in the oven and bake until the whites are a golden brown. Serve sprinkled with freshly ground black pepper. Serves 6.

What makes this egg salad different from all those other egg salads? Only two little words: crispy and crunchy. Egg salads too often tend toward mush—this one has the vegetable equivalent of backbone. Since this is made with mayonnaise, wash your hands carefully before you start to make it, and be sure to refrigerate it promptly. That's because the staphylococcus bacteria love to grow in eggs and mayonnaise, and things like that. If you have a few stray bugs on your hands, inoculate the salad, and leave it at room temperature for a couple of hours, you will be dishing out a lot of trouble for anyone who eats it. (That's how they poison forty people at the church picnics every so often.) Isn't it nice to have a cookbook written by a doctor? Medical hints along with the recipes.

Egg Salad—Traditional

SERVING TIME: 15–20 MINUTES

2 cups mayonnaise (see
   Chapter 15)
3–4 drops Tabasco sauce **or**
   ¼–½ tsp. ground chili
Freshly ground black pepper
   to taste
1 dozen hard-boiled eggs,
   sliced
1 medium onion, minced

1 medium green pepper,
   minced
2 carrots, grated (in blender
   if you wish)
½ cup finely chopped celery
½ cup grated cabbage (in
   blender)
¼ cup minced parsley
½ cup sunflower seeds

Mix the mayonnaise with the Tabasco or ground chili and ground pepper. Mix the eggs with the vegetables, seeds, and dressing, and serve on lettuce leaves. Serves 6.

10
Pasta

Once upon a time there was only one kind of pasta in the world, and it was whole-wheat pasta. That was before millions died of cancer of the colon, and before women in the major pasta-eating countries began to blow up like balloons after the age of thirty-five or so. That was in the days of high-fiber spaghetti, macaroni, lasagne, manicotti, canneloni, and virtually every other delectable baked flour noodles that cried out for a bath of tomato sauce.

Pasta made with "enriched" white flour is an obscenity, an atrocity, the humiliation of a noble dish. Devoid of fiber, deficient in usable vitamins, lacking color, flavor, and substance, it is stripped of all the virtues which it formerly possessed.

Fortunately you can restore your pasta to its position of former merit. All you have to do is make sure it is made from 100 percent stone-ground whole-wheat flour. If you can find a *truly* 100 percent whole-wheat pasta free from chemical additives, you're all set. On the other hand, making your own pasta gives you several important advantages:

1. You will taste fresh pasta for the first time in your life. It is as different from store-bought pasta as freshly baked bread is from stale commercial loaves. If you think about it, virtually all commercial pasta has gone stale, stale, stale.

2. You'll save money. Making it yourselves is cheaper than paying someone else.

3. You'll have fun. Rolling the dough through one of those gleaming pasta machines is an unspoiled old-fashioned pleasure.

4. You'll encounter a *real* convenience food. You can crank out your own spaghetti or any of a dozen other pasta forms in less than 30 minutes. Two weeks' supply can easily be made some lazy afternoon in an hour—and cooking time is a truly "instantaneous" 60 to 90 seconds.

Here are a few helpful hints to make things fast, easy, and enjoyable. The best helper of all is a top-quality mixer with a dough hook. It should cost about $100 these days, and quickly pay for itself in lower food costs and more enjoyable eating. If you can get your hands on one of these, mixing the pasta dough is a snap. You can also use an anemic name-brand electric mixer that is more a toy than a kitchen tool—and costs almost as much as a real mixer. In that case, mix the dough until your machine starts gasping, and then finish kneading by hand until the dough becomes nice and smooth. Don't try to use a hand-held electric "mixer"— you will probably fill the kitchen with smoke and flames as the wires overheat. Save those novelties for beating egg substitutes and instant mashed potatoes. A "machine" to make your own pasta runs $30 to $40 and is a lot of fun—*but you can get along fine without one.* All it actually does is roll a ball of dough into a nice even sheet. Then you pass that sheet through the rollers once again with the cutters in position. It cuts the dough into beautifully uniform strips of various sizes and shapes, and makes many varieties of pasta and noodles.

There's another equally good way to manage, however. Just roll the dough out on the tabletop, take a sharp knife and cut it into strips. Total cost for equipment: zero dollars, zero cents. It was Henry David Thoreau who said, "Beware of all enterprises that require new clothes." We say, "Beware of any recipes that require new equipment." Ours don't. You can speed things up by getting a decent mixer, a good blender, and a few other odds and ends, but you can get along without them very well. What you can't do, however, is use shoddy tools and hope to make anything decent with them.

A few words about ingredients: pasta and tomatoes live for each other. You will note that we don't use canned tomato paste or tomato "sauces." (The people who make up those aluminum envelopes think you're so dumb you can't sprinkle a few spices into a bowl. They mix the spices for you—plus a few poisonous chemicals as a bonus—and charge you $—— a pound for the privilege.) There is nothing that tastes better in a tomato sauce than a nice fresh tomato.

This is also the time to use olive oil. We prefer the cheapest brand of virgin oil, which carries the strongest flavor of the olive. For sauces, it's really delightful. Let the sauces cook under low heat as long as you can manage. The recipe says "20 to 45" minutes," but that's if you're in a hurry. An hour and a half can only make things better.

Can you get fat on pasta? I don't really think so, provided you consume only 100 percent whole-wheat pasta *as part of the high-fiber diet.* There are several good reasons for that, including the fact that this authentic pasta fills you so much that you simply lose the capacity to overeat. Beyond that you are getting all the familiar benefits of the high-fiber diet: decreased intestinal absorption, lower cholesterol, and protection from the six major diseases of civilization.

High-fiber pasta allows you to eat the food that made Italy great—instead of the starchy noodles that made America fat. Go to it.

Recipes

This is the key recipe for making your own pasta. If you knead it by hand, be sure not to knead it too little. If you knead it by machine, don't knead it too much. Now, forward march!

Homemade Pasta with Eggs—Traditional

SERVING TIME: 5–7 MINUTES

3–3½ cups stone-ground whole-wheat flour (approx.)	2 tbsps. olive oil
5 eggs, slightly beaten	2–3 tbsps. water

Put about 2 cups of the flour on a board or counter, make a hole in the middle of the flour, and pour in the beaten eggs, olive oil, and water. Gradually work the flour into the liquid, using as much flour as you need to make a good stiff dough. Knead a little so that the dough will be smooth. If you have a mixer with a dough hook, put ingredients into a mixing bowl, and let the mixer mix and knead the dough. Knead only until dough forms a smooth ball-like mass. Remove dough from bowl, shape into a ball, and leave on board covered with a towel a few minutes, then proceed with the instructions for specific type of pasta.

Economy Pasta—Traditional

SERVING TIME: 5–7 MINUTES

3½–4 cups stone-ground whole-wheat flour

2 tbsps. olive oil
1½ cups water (approx.)

Put the flour on a board or counter. Make a well in the middle and pour in the oil and ½ cup water. Gradually work the liquid into the flour, using only as much additional water as you need to make a stiff, smooth dough. Knead the dough a little. Then shape into a ball and cover for a few minutes.

For Spaghetti: Slice a piece of dough from the dough ball, roll very thin, about ⅛ inch, on a well-floured board or counter, keeping the piece of dough well-floured on top also as you roll. Roll the sheet of dough into a long roll and slice crosswise, 1/16th to 1/8th of an inch in width. Unroll the strips and lay them out on towels or on cookie sheets to dry about an hour.
ALLOW ANY OF THESE KINDS OF PASTA TO DRY ABOUT AN HOUR BEFORE COOKING.
For Fettucine: Follow the directions for spaghetti but slice diagonally ¼ of an inch to ⅜ of an inch in width.
For Manicotti: Cut dough into parallelograms of 3 inches wide by 4 inches long.
For Lasagne: Cut dough strips as long as your baking pan and about 2½ inches wide.
For Ravioli: Cut dough into 2-inch-wide strips. Makes about 100 ravioli.

If you want to save time, you can speed up the drying process by putting the pasta on cookie sheets in a 200-degree oven. In a few minutes, the pasta will be dry and ready to store in either a jar or a plastic bag. But use it quickly or it will get stale, like the stuff they sell in the store.

🔥🔥

Especially these days there are few times when you get something for nothing, but this recipe for tomato sauce gives you a free bonus: iron. According to R. S. Goodhart in *Modern Nutrition in Health and Disease*,* tomato sauce cooked in a cast-iron utensil absorbs meaningful amounts of iron, taking the place, in many cases, of expensive iron medication. Iron is of course absorbed by nearly all foods cooked in iron containers, and supplies that mineral in abundance to those who can't afford expensive and fashionable stainless steel. Ironically, the high-fashion enamel-coated iron in "decorator colors" loses all of these virtues. For this sauce, use only fresh ingredients, including crushed fresh basil leaves and fresh garlic. It's even better if you can let the sauce incubate overnight in the refrigerator before reheating it. Yum-yum.

Basic Tomato Sauce—Traditional

SERVING TIME: 7–10 MINUTES

4 pounds fresh ripe tomatoes	2 bay leaves
3 tbsps. olive oil	¼ tsp. crushed fennel seed
3–4 cloves garlic, minced	1 tsp. freshly ground black
3 onions, chopped	pepper
2 tbsps. crushed basil leaves	Juice of half a lemon

Put the tomatoes into the blender and liquefy. In a large frying pan sauté the garlic and onions in the olive oil. Add the tomatoes, basil, bay leaves, fennel seed, black pepper, and lemon juice. Let the sauce simmer until it thickens and the flavors have blended. This takes 20–45 minutes. Makes about 6½ cups of sauce.

* Fifth edition, Philadelphia, Lea and Febiger, 1973.

Quick and Easy (SERVING TIME: 2 MINUTES)
This sauce is easy to make any time. If you make it in advance it is ready for any occasion. Good planning makes a real difference in the variety of meals you can prepare.

Whole-wheat pasta has fiber—and fresh vegetables have fiber. So what could be better than combining the two? The last two variations given don't have any vegetable fiber, but they have a lot of flavor—and, besides, your homemade spaghetti has fiber to spare. So everything works out fine.

Spaghetti with Vegetable-Tomato Sauce— Traditional

SERVING TIME: 1 HOUR

1 recipe for pasta or economy pasta with or without eggs (pp.146-7)
6 cups tomato sauce (1 recipe Basic Tomato Sauce, p.148)
1 medium eggplant, washed, diced with skin on, and soaked in a large pot of water to which has been added 1 tablespoon salt. Let soak about an hour. Then wash very well to remove all excess salt. The eggplant can be soaked in the evening, washed, wrapped in a towel, and kept in the refrigerator until the next day.
½ cup Romano cheese

In a large kettle put water and bring to a boil. In the meantime warm the sauce and add the diced eggplant to it, and the cheese. If the sauce seems too thick, add a bit of broth to thin it. Cook the spaghetti about 2 minutes in the boiling water. Drain and serve smothered in the sauce and sprinkled with more cheese, if desired. You can produce a wonderful variety of sauces by adding one of the following to the basic tomato sauce and proceeding as in the recipe above.

Variations:
· Substitute for eggplant 1½ pounds of zucchini, scrubbed and sliced in rounds.
· Substitute for eggplant 1 pound fresh mushrooms, washed, sliced, and sautéed in 1 tablespoon olive oil until the liquid disappears.
· *Add* 2 green peppers, chopped, in combination with any of the above.
· Substitute for eggplant a whole, raw cauliflower cut into little flowerets and added to the sauce, without precooking it.
· Substitute for eggplant 1 medium raw cabbage, shredded, and add to the sauce.
· Substitute for eggplant approximately 1½ pounds of any combination of vegetables which will please your family.
· Of course, a meat sauce is fine. Fry 1½ pounds lean ground beef or pork, or a combination, and substitute for the eggplant.
· *Add* 1½ pounds shelled, cooked shrimp to any previous combination of vegetables.

🌀🌀

Some experts on pasta—all Italians, of course—say that simply forming the dough into different sizes and shapes gives the same dough different flavors. Personally we think they're right, but you have to be the judge. Here's another interesting little tidbit. If you sprinkle freshly ground—in your blender—hot red peppers over your pasta, in whatever form, *you will be adding a source of vitamin C 250 percent more concentrated than fresh orange juice.* That's something you'll never see on a TV commercial.

Cannelloni and Manicotti—Traditional

SERVING TIME: 1 HOUR

Cannelloni and manicotti are only slightly different in size and shape. Follow the directions for Homemade Pasta with Eggs (p. 146) and follow the specific cutting directions. (One recipe makes about 16 manicotti and 20–24 cannelloni.) After they have been cut, let them dry for an hour. In the meantime make one or two of the fillings described under Raviolis. (You will need 1½ times the filling recipes for 16 manicotti and about the same for the 20–24 cannelloni.)

Bring a large pot or kettle of water to a boil. Drop in several of the dried cannelloni or manicotti. Cook about 2–3 minutes and remove with a slotted spoon. Carefully lay the cooked pasta on a board or plate, fill with filling, roll, and lay side by side in a rectangular baking pan or Pyrex dish. Cover with your favorite tomato-vegetable, tomato-meat or tomato-shrimp sauce, as described under variations of Spaghetti with Vegetable-Tomato Sauce (p.149) or just use the Basic Tomato Sauce (p.148). Put in a preheated 375-degree oven for about 25 minutes.

Lasagne made with pasty, starchy "enriched" white flour is awful. Lasagne made with springy, tasty 100 percent whole-wheat pasta is a revelation! Don't be afraid to try the variations, especially the eggplant-and-green-pepper version—sensational! High-fiber lasagne isn't a one-dish meal—it's a one-dish feast. After you try it, you will agree, as your family sits there grinning from ear to ear.

Lasagne—Traditional

SERVING TIME: 1 HOUR

Dough: ½ recipe Homemade Pasta with Eggs (p.146)
Meatballs:
1½ pounds ground meat (A mixture of pork and beef is very good, preferably ground at home.)
2 tsps. crushed basil
¼ tsp. crushed hot peppers
¼ tsp. crushed fennel seed
3 tsps. olive oil
2 cloves garlic, peeled and minced

Mix the meat with the basil, hot peppers, and fennel seed. Make into marble-sized meatballs. In the olive oil fry the garlic for a minute or so. Add the meatballs and brown. Drain the meatballs.

Basic Tomato Sauce: About 4 cups (p. 148)

Cheese Filling:
2 *pounds fresh ricotta*
2 *eggs*
¼ *cup chopped parsley* **or**
  2 *tbsps. parsley flakes*
½ *cup grated Parmesan or*
  Romano cheese

½ *tsp. freshly ground black*
  pepper
1 *pound mozzarella, thinly*
  sliced

In a mixing bowl mix well ricotta, eggs, parsley, Parmesan or Romano, and black pepper. Slice mozzarella. In a large 8–10-quart kettle bring water to a boil and gently boil the pasta about 2 minutes. Drain.

In a large rectangular baking dish at least 2 inches deep put ½ cup of tomato sauce. Then place a layer of noodles (about 4), then, in layers, half the meatballs, half the ricotta cheese filling, half the mozzarella slices and 1 cup more of tomato sauce. Add another layer of noodles, ½ cup tomato sauce, remaining meatballs, remaining ricotta mixture, remaining slices of mozzarella, 1 cup tomato sauce, and top with another layer of noodles. Pour over the top layer of noodles another ½–1 cup tomato sauce.

Place the lasagne in a preheated 350-degree oven and bake 20–30 minutes. Before cutting into squares, let stand a few minutes to cool a little to make the cutting easier. Serves 6.

Quick and Easy (SERVING TIME: 15 MINUTES)
When you plan ahead just a tiny bit you can create a masterpiece in a few minutes. The tomato sauce can be something that you keep on hand, and so is ready when you need it. Also, the pasta can be made in advance. While you are assembling the lasagne ingredients, you can be bringing the water to a boil to cook the lasagne. Also, the meat could be fried and drained and kept in the refrigerator until the day of assembling. I would suggest preparing the meat the day before you want it. And the tomato sauce can easily be made up as much as a week before. The cheese and

eggs should be assembled on the spot. The actual putting-together only takes a few minutes.

Variations:
• Try a combination of eggplant, green peppers, and zucchini, about 1½ pounds in total, added to the sauce instead of the meat. About an hour before or the night before, the eggplant should be washed and cubed with the skin on, and put in a large pot of water to which has been added 1 tablespoon salt. Let soak. Drain and wash well to remove excess salt. Dry with a towel. Use immediately or wrap in a dry towel and store in refrigerator until the next day. The squash can be diced or sliced on the spot.
• Instead of meat, try any of the vegetable combinations suggested under Spaghetti with Vegetable-Tomato Sauce.

"Sou-Beoreg" (su-boor-egg) can be considered Armenian lasagne. On the other hand, lasagne can be considered Italian Sou-Beoreg. It all depends on how you want to look at it. But either way, it's a fine, hearty dish. Make sure the cheese is first quality, and you will be well repaid.

Sou-Beoreg or Armenian Cheese Lasagne— Traditional

SERVING TIME: 30–40 MINUTES

Dough:

2 cups stone-ground whole-wheat flour
3 eggs

2 tbsps. olive oil
A little water to make a firm dough

Place the flour on a board or counter, make a well in the middle, and break the eggs into the well. Also put the olive oil into the well, and gradually begin to knead the liquid into the flour. Add a little water, if needed, to make a firm dough ball. Knead the dough until it is smooth. Cover the dough well with a towel while you prepare the filling.

Cheese Filling:

2 *pounds fresh ricotta cheese*
4 *eggs*
1 *tsp. freshly ground black pepper*

2 *pounds grated Muenster cheese (can be grated in blender)*
½ *cup chopped parsley*

In a large bowl mix the above ingredients together.

Cooking and Assembling Sou-Beoreg:
Put a large kettle of water on to boil.

Divide the dough into 6–8 balls of equal size. Roll each one out to the size of the rectangular baking pan you are using, keeping the dough about 1/16th of an inch in thickness. Grease the baking pan. Drop the sheets of dough into the boiling water for about a minute. Remove carefully into a towel and allow to drain. When well drained, place 3 or 4 layers of noodles on the bottom of the baking pan. Cover these with the cheese filling. Place the remaining 3 or 4 sheets of noodles in layers on top of the cheese. Brush 3–4 tbsps. butter on the top layer of noodles. Bake in a preheated 400-degree oven for 20–30 minutes. Serves 6.

🐾 🦀

Ravioli are wonderful little sandwiches filled with spicy, flavorful combinations. Moreover, they are an excellent source of nutrition. If you use 100-percent whole-wheat flour (what else?) and combine two each of the cheese, vegetable, and meat ravioli, you have provided yourself with just about all the vitamins, minerals, protein, and everything else you need for that meal—and in some cases for the entire day. But even better, you have had a taste treat you'll never forget. Isn't that an offer worth taking?

Ravioli—Traditional

SERVING TIME: 1½ HOURS

*1 recipe Basic Tomato Sauce
or any variation*

*1 recipe Homemade Pasta
with Eggs (follow directions
for making dough—makes
about 200 raviolis).*

Don't roll dough until ready to fill raviolis.

Cheese Filling:

*1½ pounds ricotta cheese
¾ pound mozzarella cheese,
grated
3 eggs
⅓ cup grated Parmesan
cheese*

*⅓ cup chopped parsley
1 tsp. freshly ground black
pepper
2 tsps. crushed oregano*

Blend above ingredients together.

Meat Filling:

*¾ pound fresh spinach
1 tbsp. olive oil
2 cloves garlic, peeled and
minced
1 medium onion, peeled and
minced
1½ pounds ground meat (a
combination of beef and
pork is best)*

*⅓ cup minced parsley
⅓ cup bran (used instead of
bread crumbs)
⅓ cup grated Parmesan or
Romano cheese
3 eggs
¼ tsp. crushed hot peppers
(optional)*

Wash and cook the spinach in a covered saucepan in ½ inch water, about 5 minutes. In the meantime in a large frying pan sauté garlic and onion in the olive oil for a minute or so. Add the ground meat and parsley, and sauté until the meat is cooked. This only takes a few minutes. If you use pork, make sure it is well cooked. Drain and chop the spinach either by hand, in a food chopper, or in the blender. When the meat is cool, add the rest of the ingredients.

Variation:
Use 3 cups leftover cooked chicken, pork, or beef, finely chopped or put through a food chopper. Sauté only garlic and onion.

Vegetable Filling:

2 tbsps. olive oil
2 cloves garlic, minced
1 medium onion, minced
2 green peppers, minced
¼ pound carrots, minced
½ pound zucchini squash, minced
½ pound cabbage, finely shredded
(All the above vegetables

can be minced or shredded in blender.)
2 eggs
¼ cup minced parsley
½ cup grated Romano cheese
2 tbsps. basil
½ cup bran
½ tsp. freshly ground black pepper

In a large frying pan sauté the garlic, onion, and green peppers in olive oil, for a minute or so. Add the carrots, squash, and cabbage, and sauté another 2 minutes. Take the vegetables off the heat and let cool. When cool, mix the vegetables with the eggs, parsley, cheese, basil, bran, and black pepper.

Variation:
Use your imagination and your family's preference in approximately the same amounts indicated for a taste treat.

Quick and Easy (SERVING TIME: 45 MINUTES TO 1 HOUR)
The fillings can be made in advance. The nature of the ravioli requires that the dough be made and filled before the dough dries. If you want to fill and dry the raviolis ahead of time, they can be stored in the refrigerator in a covered container for a few days until you're ready to cook and serve them.

Making Raviolis:
When the fillings are ready, roll, and cut the dough as in the recipe for Homemade Pasta with Eggs for raviolis. On each strip of dough drop teaspoonfuls of filling every 2 inches, beginning about ½ inch in from the end of each strip. Cover with another strip of dough, press around each filling to form the square

ravioli, cut the ravioli apart, and press around the edges of each
one again with the tines of a fork to be sure that the edges are
sealed.

Leave the raviolis on baking sheets to dry at least an hour. At
this point you can cook them in a large deep pot of boiling water
about 2–3 minutes. Be sure you don't cook too many at a time.
Remove them carefully with a slotted spoon and put them in one
large or individual warm plates. Serve with tomato sauce and
top with Parmesan cheese.

The name in Chinese is "Jao Tze," the origin is Peking, and
the flavor is sensational. An exception to the rule of using
processed foods is the soy sauce. Since there is no equivalent in
American cooking, the only alternatives are to use it or do without it. It is a product that has been tested by time; its use in
China goes back about 3,000 years, more or less. If you decide
to add it, get the best-quality imported light soy sauce without
additives. Skimping on the quality of food ingredients is like
skimping on the quality of medicine—it doesn't pay. But do try
to include the Chinese sesame oil—it has a unique smoke flavor
and makes a big difference. A few drops do the trick.

Chinese Ravioli—Traditional

SERVING TIME: 45 MINUTES TO 1 HOUR

Dough:
3 cups stone-ground whole-   Approximately 1½ cups water
  wheat flour

Mix the flour with some of the water, adding as much water as
you need to make a firm dough. Knead a few minutes to make a
smooth dough ball. This makes about 4 dozen balls 1 inch in
diameter which roll into 3–3½-inch rounds.

Filling:

1 tbsp. oil	*1 tbsp. soy sauce (optional)*
4 minced green onions	*1 tbsp. minced fresh ginger*
1 pound ground pork	*½ tsp. Chinese sesame oil*
½ pound shrimp, shelled, and	*(Optional—this is a dark,*
minced	*smoky-flavored oil and is*
1½ cups finely shredded	*worth including—a little*
cabbage (shred in blender)	*goes a long way.)*

Sauté the green onions in the 1 tablespoon oil for a minute or so. Add the ground pork and shrimp, and cook until pork is well cooked, about 5–7 minutes. Add cabbage and sauté another minute or so. Remove the pork-shrimp from the heat and mix in all the other ingredients, stirring well. Drain off any excess liquid.
Stuffing Chinese raviolis:
Roll out each ball into a 3–3½-inch round. If you want, roll the dough and cut with a glass or dough cutter which is the size you want. Put about 2 teaspoons of filling on half of the round. Fold the round in half, and seal the edges by pressing them together carefully with the tines of a fork.

Bring a large kettle of water to a boil, and boil these raviolis about 2 minutes. Don't put more than a layer of raviolis in the kettle at one time. Remove them with a slotted spoon and serve hot with the following sauce. Makes 48 Jao Tze.
Sauce:

⅔ cup vinegar	*sauce to taste (You may*
2 tbsps. soy sauce	*use ordinary red pepper*
2 tbsps. Chinese sesame oil	*sauce as a substitute.)*
2–8 drops Chinese red pepper	*2 tbsps. toasted sesame seeds*

Heat all ingredients and serve hot over Jao Tze.

11

Soups

Remember the old line about how the food processors make chicken soup—"they tie a string around the chicken's neck and let him swim across a tank of hot water"? These days they don't even *have* to do that. They can soak the string in "hydrolized vegetable protein, monosodium glutamate (MSG), coconut oil, disodium guanylate, and starch" and *then* pull it through. (That's the recipe for imitation chicken flavor.)

Those canned abominations and their "dry soup mix" cousins are about as far from real soup as lightning is from a lightning bug. Instead of the best-quality vegetables, they may be made from specially selected varieties that stand up under heat and pressure. Canned and concentrated soups are processed at high temperature and pressure to destroy enzymes that could cause spoilage. Unfortunately these are the same enzymes that your body desperately needs. The processing also zaps vitamins and other vital nutritional components, as well as impairing the fiber content of the final product. It's hard to see—if you think it through—why anyone ever eats that kind of "soup."

Look at it this way. Those big soup companies buy the same vegetables that are available to you, overprocess them, add hazardous chemicals, and sell them back to you at insane prices. The outrageous price tags include the cost of high-pressure advertising to convince you of the following untruths:
1. Their vegetables are better than yours—"fresher," "peak of perfection," and other nonsense.
2. Canned or dry soups are good for your children. You know, all those smiling faces guzzling soup laced with brain-impairing

MSG? Canned soups are defective nutritionally compared to fresh homemade soup.

3. Canned and dry soups are somehow "convenient." The soup manufacturers believe that most Americans are too stupid to heat water and add ingredients. They also believe that we have the taste buds of a wart hog with a bad cold. Paying 30¢ for a can of soup only means that you have to do without something else or that you have to work harder to replace the money that never had to be spent in the first place.

They *don't* try to tell you their soups are cheap or safe. Not too long ago a major specialty soup company went out of business because a big part of their product was contaminated with lethal botulism toxin. From time to time there are hasty "recalls" of major brands of canned and dry soups and not because they put in a little too much salt, you can be sure.

Now, if you make your own soup you will save a lot of money, avoid the risk of botulism, keep dangerous chemicals out of your body, increase your fiber intake, and most important of all, experience some unmatchable flavors. The process of making soup at *home* is unique. It is based on the concept of extracting the flavor, by gentle heating, from each ingredient. Thus if you like corn, a corn soup should be the quintessence of corn flavor, with all the delicate shading and nuances. (Commercial soups can't do that because they require much more intense processing and are shotgunned with cheap flavoring agents to cover up the drab taste.)

Beyond that, many of the soup recipes that follow are really one-dish meals. The Bean Sprout Soup, for example, and the White on White Bean Soup with chorizo comprise a meal that literally cooks itself. Another bonus these days is that emphasizing homemade soup will really cut your food costs. You can cut back on your meat purchases, avoid expensive processed foods, almost completely, and have a great time while you're doing it. And don't forget, homemade bread goes great with every kind of soup.

Recipes

Please don't give your kids bouillon cubes. You can eat them yourself if you want to, but salt in large amounts is poison to developing bodies. Most physicians agree that high salt intake is one of the major causes of high blood pressure. Actually you should cut your own salt intake to a minimum, but you already know that. Your kids, on the other hand, have to eat pretty much what you give them. Bouillon cubes, bouillon powder, canned consommé, and dry soup mixes are mostly salt (cheap ingredient) with a lot of chemicals that have no place in the human body. If you want the convenience they offer, just freeze your own soup stock in an ice-cube tray and add a cube or two when the recipe calls for "soup stock." Cheaper, better quality, and better taste. What more could you ask for?

Beef Stock—Traditional

SERVING TIME: 5 MINUTES

2 pounds beef or veal knuckle
2 marrow bones
2 pounds shin of beef
4 pounds lean brisket
5 quarts water
4 medium leeks, sliced down
the center lengthwise, and
washed well
3 large peeled onions, studded
with one clove each
3 stalks of celery, with leaves

4 large carrots
4 sprigs parsley
2 white turnips, quartered
2 beets, quartered (optional)
2 green peppers, seeded and
quartered
6 peppercorns
3 cloves garlic, halved
2 bay leaves
½ tsp. thyme
½ tsp. marjoram

In a large 8 10-quart soup kettle put the beef or veal knuckle, marrow bones, shin of beef, and brisket. Cover with water and bring to a boil. Remove the scum as it accumulates on the surface. Now add the vegetables and spices. Continue to skim off the scum that rises until there is none. Cover lightly and simmer gently for 4–5 hours. Strain the liquid through a very fine strainer or a double thickness of cheesecloth. Use the meat in spaghetti sauce, for lasagne, sauce on tortillas or chapatis, with a piquant tomato sauce, or topped with the cabbage salad. Or try chalupas. Use the vegetables, liquefied, and add to sauces or soups to thicken. Makes 4 quarts.

🐟🐟

You can use a stewing chicken for this recipe—it even makes it better. If you read the label on the "chicken-flavored" bouillon products, you'll see that chicken is often not the first ingredient mentioned. As U.S. law requires the ingredients to be listed in order of predominance (main ingredient first, etc.) you can see that chicken is a minority stockholder in most commercial "chicken" products. Things got so bad a while back that the government had to step in and establish minimum quantities of chicken in "chicken" products. For example, "chicken soup" has to contain *at least* a big *2 percent* chicken! How would you like to ride on tires that contained 2 percent rubber while paying for the real thing?

Chicken Stock—Traditional

SERVING TIME: 5 MINUTES

1 4–5 pound chicken
4 chicken feet, cleaned
   (optional)
1–2 veal knuckle bones
5 quarts water
5–6 leeks, split lengthwise, and
   cleaned
2 large onions, one studded
   with 3 cloves
4 stalks of celery with leaves
6–8 peppercorns
4 large carrots

4 sprigs of parsley
1 turnip, quartered
2 summer squash, cut in
   several large pieces
2 green peppers, quartered
3 cloves garlic
1 bay leaf
½ tsp. thyme
½ tsp. sage
½ small cabbage, cut in
   quarters

In a large 8–10-quart kettle or soup pot put the chicken, chicken feet (if you can find them), veal knuckle bones, and water. Bring the water to a boil, and skim off all the scum. Add the vegetables and spices and simmer gently, partially covered, about 2 hours. Strain the stock through a fine sieve or double thickness of cheese-cloth. Cool and skim off the fat. Store in refrigerator. Use the chicken in soups, salads, in sauces. Try chalupas on page 00. The vegetables can be puréed and used to thicken sauces or soups. Makes 4½ quarts.

Make sure the avocado is soft—so you can dent it with your finger. To keep it from turning brown—secret of Incas: put avocado seed into mixture until ready to use. Small portions of this superb soup will enhance your reputation as a gourmet cook.

Cold Avocado Soup—Traditional

SERVING TIME: 10 MINUTES

1 quart chicken stock
3 cups mashed avocado (ripe
   avocados, halved, peeled,
   and pitted)
Juice of a lemon
1 clove garlic
¼ tsp. freshly ground black
   pepper

Pinch of cayenne pepper to
   taste
½ cup half and half
Grate in blender: 1 turnip and
   3 carrots
Chopped chives **or** green
   onions

Heat the chicken stock, and mix in the avocado, lemon juice, and garlic. Blend this in blender. Season the soup with the pepper and cayenne pepper. Add half and half. Blend again a few seconds. Chill. Serve sprinkled with a couple of tablespoons of the grated turnips, carrots, and chopped green onions or chives, mixed together. Serves 6.

Remember, whenever it comes to broth—beef or chicken—you'll do best to make your own. You'll find our favorite recipes on pp.161-2, but feel free to improvise. The commercial broths are *there*—that's about the best one can say for them. The quality varies from fair to ghastly, and they have too much salt. Some of them have other *unexciting* additions to your diet like monosodium glutamate. Stay away from those.

Yogurt and egg plus barley and mint are a superb combination of flavors—and give you everything you ever want as far as the benefits of the high-fiber diet are concerned. Go to it.

Barley-Mint Soup—Traditional

SERVING TIME: 5 MINUTES

1 tbsp. butter	¼ cup chopped fresh parsley,
1 large onion, chopped	**or** 2 tbsps. dried parsley
4 cups beef or chicken stock	¼ cup chopped fresh mint,
1 cup barley	**or** 2 tbsps. crushed dried
3 cups yogurt	mint
1 egg	

In a small frying pan sauté the onion in the butter. In a 2½–3-quart saucepan bring the stock to a boil. Add the onion mixture. Add the barley, bring to a boil, and simmer for about 20 minutes. Beat the yogurt and egg together. Put 1 tablespoon broth into the yogurt-egg mixture, and then carefully add the mixture to the rest of the broth. Heat, stirring, but do not boil. When ready to serve add the parsley and mint. Serve in deep bowls. Serves 4–6.

There's no reason not to grow the bean sprouts yourself—it will also give you something to fall back on in case of atomic attack, power failure, or forgetting to have your husband or wife pick something up on the way home from work. The water chestnuts and bamboo shoots are available in cans—not much choice there, unless you happen to have a bamboo grove at the edge of a running stream. This dish is so good that words just can't describe it.

Bean Sprout Soup—Traditional

SERVING TIME: 10 MINUTES

½ cup dried mushrooms **or**
  1 cup fresh, sliced mushrooms
1 tbsp. oil
Small piece pork fat
2 cloves garlic, minced
1 cup chopped onions
½ cup chopped green onions
½ cup chopped celery
½ pound ground pork

2 quarts chicken **or** beef stock
3 cups bean sprouts
½ cup water chestnuts
½ cup bamboo shoots
½ cup fresh peas
1 tbsp. soy sauce
1 tbsp. molasses
1 cup whole-wheat noodles
More chopped green onions
  for topping

If you use dried mushrooms, put them in a bowl, cover them with warm water, and let them stand about 15 minutes while you prepare the rest of the soup. Put oil in a 4–5-quart pot and fry the pork fat. In the rendered fat sauté garlic, onions, celery, and ground pork for a few minutes. Add the stock, vegetables, chopped reconstituted mushrooms (if you used that kind) or the fresh mushrooms, soy sauce, molasses, and noodles. Simmer the soup about 10 minutes. Serve with some more chopped green onions sprinkled on top. Serves 6.

🦞🦞

This is the dish that proves black is beautiful—also full of fiber, sensationally delicious, and totally balanced in food elements. The "secret ingredient" is the cloves, and the half a pig's foot doesn't do any harm either. Try it hot from the oven with whole-wheat bread and fresh butter or, traditionally, over Mexican-style brown rice. Uhmm! Just as soon as I finish writing this, I'm going to have some.

Black Bean Soup—Traditional

SERVING TIME: 7 MINUTES

1 tbsp. olive oil
Half a pig's foot
3 cloves garlic, minced
2 medium onions, chopped
2 medium green peppers,
  chopped

2 cups dried black beans
2½ quarts water
¼ tsp. ground cloves
⅛ tsp. nutmeg
3 tbsps. olivy-tasting olive oil

In a 3–3½-quart pot brown half a pig's foot in 1 tablespoon olive oil. Add the garlic, onions, green peppers, dried beans, water, cloves, and nutmeg. Bring the water to a boil, lower the heat to simmer, cover and cook about 2½–3½ hours, depending on beans, stirring occasionally. When you're ready to serve the soup add the 3 tablespoons olive oil and mix it well into the soup, simmer another minute or so. Serve in deep bowl. Serves 6.

🔥🔥

You know, the colors in this dish are really beautiful—the white beans, the pale orange carrots, the bright green peppers. Crush the rosemary leaves and bay leaf together just before you put them in—you'll get the most flavor that way. (But you knew that already.) This really isn't a soup at all but what the Spanish and Latin Americans call a "caldo." It's a thick combination of beans and vegetables with a superb flavor that makes a fine main dish. You can add *good quality sausage*—no nitrates or nitrites or other poison—to any of these caldos. Look for the Spanish type called "chorizo," if you can make sure it's free of contamination with chemicals. If not, you can make your own very easily—at half the price. See p. 79.

White on White Bean Soup—Traditional

SERVING TIME: 10 MINUTES

2 tbsps. butter
2 medium onions, chopped
2 medium green peppers,
  chopped
6 cups beef **or** chicken stock
½ cup white beans
½ cup soy beans

½ cup chickpeas
3 carrots, diced
1 bay leaf
1 tsp. crushed rosemary
½ tsp. freshly ground pepper
¼ cup buckwheat

In a 2½–3-quart pot sauté onions and green peppers in butter for a few minutes. Add the stock, beans, chickpeas, carrots, bay leaf, rosemary, black pepper, and buckwheat, and simmer for 2 hours. Serves 6.

Lentils are delicate little legumes—the plant itself has lovely pale blue flowers. But don't let the esthetics fool you. Each lentil is a nutritional powerhouse packed with fiber, protein, and potassium. Put them together with cracked wheat, chickpeas, toss in the mint, garlic, and oregano, and stand back! Great things are about to happen!

Lentil–Cracked-Wheat Soup—Traditional

SERVING TIME: 5 MINUTES

1 tbsp. butter
1 clove garlic, minced
1 medium onion, chopped
8 cups chicken stock
½ cup lentils
½ cup cracked wheat
½ cup chickpeas

½ tsp. freshly ground black
  pepper
2 tbsps. fresh mint, **or** 1 tsp.
  crushed dried mint
1 tsp. oregano
1 tsp. crushed cumin seeds

In a 2½–3-quart pot sauté garlic and onion in butter for a minute or so. Add the stock, lentils, cracked wheat, chickpeas, ground black pepper, mint, oregano, and cumin. Bring to a boil and simmer, covered, for 1–1½ hours, stirring frequently. Serves 6.

🌿 🔥

Keep the green beans crunchy, the lentils tender, and you will be delighted with the results. The curry seems to hold all the other ingredients together—and then lets them go their own way after the first 4 or 5 spoonfuls.

Curried Lentil-Green Soup—Traditional

SERVING TIME: 15–20 MINUTES

1 tbsp. butter	1 tbsp. Madras curry powder
2 cloves garlic, minced	Juice of half a lemon
1 large onion, chopped	¼ tsp. ground black pepper
5 cups beef or chicken stock	2 cups green beans, chopped
1 cup lentils	1 cup mustard greens, or
1 tsp. chervil	chopped spinach

In a 3-quart pot sauté the garlic and onion in the butter for a minute or so. Add the stock, lentils, chervil, curry, lemon juice, and black pepper. Simmer for half an hour. Add the green beans and mustard greens, and simmer another 5–7 minutes. This will leave the green beans with a crunch. Serves 6.

🌿 🔥

Canned pea soup has always reminded me—for some reason— of canned smog. Hyped up with the usual commercial flavorings, chemicals, and the obligatory slug of salt, it is hazardous to one's palate. This soup is a different story. Dried peas are the incarnation of the essence of the delicate "tender little pea" flavor. The spices and the garlic make this a delicate—but fiber-filled—dish.

Split Pea Soup—Traditional

SERVING TIME: 10 MINUTES

Small piece of pork fat (about
  2 x 2 inches)
2 medium onions, coarsely
  chopped
2 stalks celery, coarsely
  chopped **or** ½ tsp. celery
  seeds
2 cloves garlic, minced

¼ cup chopped parsley
5 cups chicken stock
1½ cups split peas
4 carrots, coarsely chopped
½ tsp. marjoram
½ tsp. basil
1 cup chopped green onions

In a 3-quart pot fry the pork fat until crisp. Remove the pork fat and sauté the onions, celery, garlic, and parsley in the rendered fat about a minute or so. Add the stock, split peas, carrots, marjoram, and basil, and simmer about an hour and a half, stirring occasionally. Blend the soup (2 cups at a time) in the blender and serve sprinkled with the green onions. Serves 6.

Every kernel of tender corn has a big drop of white, fragrant "corn milk" within it. That's what comes out in the flavor of this nice soup. A word of advice—don't use "chili powder" if you can possibly avoid. Most of the mixtures are appalling. I found one the other day that contained "sodium silicate." In that, fellow victims, is nothing more or less than SAND. So look for the "powdered chili" in the little plastic bags in your market; adjust the amount to your taste. Now where do you get the whole-wheat cheese croutons? You turn to p.211 and follow the recipe, that's how.

Corn Chowder—Traditional

SERVING TIME: 20–25 MINUTES

2 tbsps. butter
2 medium onions, chopped
2 medium green peppers,
  chopped
2 medium tomatoes, chopped
2 quarts chicken stock
5 cups freshly cut corn kernels
5 cups diced potatoes (5 large)

½ tsp. freshly ground black
  pepper
1 tsp. oregano
2 tsps. ground chili
2 tsps. crushed cumin seeds
  or 1 tbsp. chili powder
2 cups mustard greens,
  chopped

In a 4½–5-quart pot sauté the onions and green peppers in the butter for a minute or so. Add the tomatoes and sauté another minute. Add the chicken stock, corn kernels, potatoes, spices, and greens, bring to a boil, and simmer 15 minutes. Top each bowl with whole-wheat cheese croutons. Serves 6–8.

🐚🐚

Cucumbers are a problem, unfortunately. Pick fresh firm ones and *scrub* with hot water, soap, and a brush. They have more wax on them these days than a suburban kitchen floor in one of those tacky floor-wax commercials. The skin is high in fiber and a nice part of the vegetable, but if you can't get the wax off, then give up and peel off the skin. "Ice cold" means as cold as you can manage—that's what makes the difference.

Cold Cucumber Soup—Traditional

SERVING TIME: 5 MINUTES

5 cups yogurt
2 cups ice water
3 cucumbers with skin, diced
  (Wash well in warm water
  and soap to remove wax.)

⅓ cup chopped green onions
Freshly ground black pepper
⅓ cup chopped parsley
3 tbsps. freshly chopped dill

In a deep bowl put the yogurt and mix in the ice water, cucumbers, green onions, and black pepper. Let chill well in the refrigerator for a few hours or add ice cubes to chill it quickly. When ready to serve, sprinkle with the fresh parsley and dill, and serve in deep bowls.

🐝 🐟

Ah, gazpacho, what crimes are committed in thy name! Keep it simple, fresh, and topped with finely diced vegetables. A sprinkle of powdered chili—not chili powder—and who could ask for more? High fiber in a cool and elegant way.

Gazpacho—Traditional

SERVING TIME: 5 MINUTES

4 *large tomatoes, cut in*
   eighths
2 *medium green peppers,*
   chopped
1 *medium sweet onion,*
   chopped

2 *medium cucumbers,*
   chopped
¼ *cup olive oil*
¼ *cup vinegar*
2 *cloves garlic*
Cayenne pepper to taste

In a blender put all the ingredients, cover, and blend.
Prepare the following:

1 *small cucumber, minced*
1 *small green pepper, minced*

1 *small sweet onion, minced*
1 *small tomato, diced*

Serve the gazpacho ice-cold in deep bowls sprinkled with some of each of the diced vegetables. Serves 6–8.

🐝 🐟

Chickpeas are magnificent vegetables. They have as much protein as sirloin steak! (A word here about protein. Some "nutritionists" pontificate that vegetables like beans don't compare with meat as a source of protein because the protein is not "complete." That means it doesn't have all the essential amino acids. We say—very rationally and scientifically—so what? The odds and ends of missing amino acids find their way into your body via milk, cheese, or meat that you consume during the day. So just enjoy it.)

Garbanzo-Vegetable Soup—Traditional

SERVING TIME: 20–25 MINUTES

Small piece of pork fat (about
  2 x 2 inches)
3 cloves garlic, minced
1 pound ground pork
1 cup chickpeas
9 cups chicken stock
4 carrots, diced or rounds
2 leeks, washed and chopped
1 pound potatoes, diced

3 cups chopped cabbage
1 cup chopped celery
2 cups chopped green beans
1 cup chopped zucchini
½ cup washed brown rice
½ tsp. black pepper, freshly
  ground
2 tbsps. Madras curry powder
2 cups whole-wheat noodles

In a 4½–5-quart pot fry the piece of pork fat. In the rendered fat sauté the garlic. Then sauté the ground pork for a few minutes. Add the chickpeas and chicken stock and cook 2 hours. Now add the carrots, leeks, potatoes, cabbage, celery, green beans, zucchini, rice, black pepper, and Madras curry powder. Cook another 20 minutes. Add the noodles and cook 5 minutes more. Serve in deep bowls. Serves 6–8.

Caldo Gallego has been a classic of Spanish cuisine for over a thousand years. It is the personification of everything that is fine and noble about the culture: solid, honest, powerful. Nutritionally it is a dish beyond compare—and provides overwhelming gratification to the eater. It thrives on the addition of the Spanish sausage called "chorizo." If you can find good quality chorizo nitrate- and nitrite-free and otherwise bereft of poisons, by all means add it. If not, make your own, following the recipe on p. 79. If you have to leave it out, think about putting it in next time. It's worth it.

Caldo Gallego, High-Fiber Version—Traditional

SERVING TIME: 20 MINUTES

Small piece of pork fat (about 2 x 2 inches)
1 pound ground pork
1 pig's foot
3 cloves garlic, minced
4 onions, chopped
1 cup chickpeas (garbanzo beans)
1 cup soy beans
2 quarts water
½ medium head cabbage, coarsely chopped

1 pound potatoes, diced (2 large)
3 turnips, diced
3 tomatoes, chopped
2 tbsps. crushed cumin seeds
1 tsp. crushed hot red pepper
½ tsp. freshly ground black pepper
½ pound mustard greens
1½ pounds chorizo (optional)

In a 5-quart saucepan or kettle fry the piece of pork fat. In the rendered fat fry the ground pork and the pig's foot with the garlic. Add the onions and sauté a bit more. Now add the chickpeas (garbanzos), soy beans, and water and simmer, covered, about 2 hours. At this time add the cabbage, potatoes, turnips, and tomatoes with the cumin, hot red pepper, and black pepper. Simmer about 15 minutes more. Add the greens and simmer about 5 minutes more. Serve in deep bowls. Serves 8–10.

(Important note: If you do use the chorizo, fry it separately and drain. Add just before serving.)

🌿🌿

Remember those courses in "music appreciation" back in high school? Well, this soup is a course in "vegetable appreciation." You can vary the ingredients, but keep the proportions about the same. Watch the sizes of the dice—don't make everything the same-size little cube or it will have the look and feel—but not the taste—of those little cans of (ugh!) "condensed vegetable soup."

Hearty High-Fiber Vegetable Soup—Traditional

SERVING TIME: 20–25 MINUTES

4 tbsps. butter
2 cups chopped onions
3 cloves garlic, minced
2 large green peppers,
  chopped
2½ quarts beef or chicken
  stock
2 large tomatoes, chopped
1 cup diced carrots
2 cups chopped cabbage
1 cup diced turnips
1 cup diced beets
1 cup diced potatoes
1 cup freshly grated corn

1 cup diced squash
1 cup diced celery
2 cups chopped green beans
1½ cups barley
Juice of a lemon
1 bay leaf
½ tsp. freshly ground black
  pepper
2 tsps. marjoram
1 tsp. thyme
¼–½ tsp. crushed hot peppers
  or more to taste
½ cup chopped parsley

In a 4½–5-quart pot sauté the onions, garlic, and green peppers in the butter about 2 minutes. Add the stock and the vegetables, barley, lemon juice, and spices—except the parsley. Cover and simmer about 20 minutes. Add the parsley and simmer another 3 minutes. Serves 6–8.

Minestrone is not "just vegetable soup with an Italian name." It is Italy disguised as vegetable soup. It has charm and "brio," and romance—and a touch of tragedy because it gets eaten so fast. It also has fiber without limit, protein in abundance, and enough flavor for a family of twelve. But be sure to use whole-wheat pasta—that's what the original recipe, 300 years old, calls for.

Remember, in those days whole wheat was the only kind of wheat. And cancer was just the Latin name for a crab.

Minestrone—Traditional

SERVING TIME: 20–25 MINUTES

¼ cup olive oil
3 cloves garlic, minced
2 medium onions, chopped
2 medium green peppers, chopped
1 cup diced celery with leaves
2 cups shredded cabbage
2 zucchini squash, diced
2 cups diced carrots
¼ cup chopped parsley
2 large tomatoes, chopped

½ cup kidney or pinto beans
½ cup white beans
⅓ cup brown rice
2 quarts chicken or beef stock
1 tbsp. crushed sage
1 tbsp. crushed sweet basil
1 tsp. crushed fennel seed
Freshly ground pepper
1 cup whole-wheat macaroni or noodles
1 cup Parmesan cheese

In a 3–3½-quart pot sauté the garlic, onions, green peppers, celery, cabbage, squash, carrots, and parsley in the olive oil for a few minutes. Add the tomatoes and sauté another minute or so. Add the beans, rice, stock, sage, basil, fennel, and ground pepper. Simmer the soup about 2 hours. Add the noodles and simmer another 5 minutes. Mix in the Parmesan cheese and serve. Serves 6–8.

Vichyssoise is fragile, delicate, and elegant. It's rich, but you don't have to eat very much at one time—and by the third day the flavors will have blended superbly. The fiber should dispel any evil influence of the cream.

High-Fiber Curried Vichyssoise

SERVING TIME: 20 MINUTES

2 tbsps. butter
4 leeks, sliced and washed
 well, including the green
 part
3 medium potatoes, scrubbed
 and quartered
1 cup chopped cabbage

2 medium turnips, quartered
5 cups chicken stock
1 tbsp. Madras curry powder
⅛ tsp. nutmeg
2 cups half and half
Minced parsley
Minced green onions

In a 3–3½-quart pot sauté the leeks in the butter until lightly browned. Add the potatoes, with their skins, cut in quarters, cabbage, turnips, stock, curry, and nutmeg. Simmer about 20 minutes. Blend 2 cups at a time in the blender, stir in the half and half, and chill. Serve topped with parsley and green onions. Serves 6–8.

From the land of the Creoles comes "Quin Bombo"—known in the supermarket as "okra." But pick the smallest, tenderest pods you can find—two inches long is dandy. This fine soup can be reheated the next day—but I don't know how it would taste then, since there's never been any left over at our house.

Quin Bombo Soup—Traditional

SERVING TIME: 20 MINUTES

2 tbsps. butter
3 large onions, chopped
2 green peppers, chopped
2 quarts beef or chicken stock
6 large tomatoes, chopped
2 pounds fresh okra, cut in
 thirds

¼ cup freshly chopped parsley
½ tsp. freshly ground black
 pepper
½ tsp. thyme
½ tsp. marjoram
Juice of 1 lemon
Parmesan cheese

In a large 3–3½-quart pot sauté the onions and green peppers in the butter. Add the stock, tomatoes, okra, parsley, pepper, thyme, marjoram, and lemon juice. Bring to a boil, lower heat, cover, and let simmer about 20 minutes. Serve sprinkled with Parmesan cheese if desired. Serves 6.

12
Salads

For the American homemaker a very practical problem is just getting enough fiber into the family diet. Decades of brainwashing have made her husband and children—and perhaps even her—resistant to the idea of eating fresh, high-fiber vegetables. When was the last time you saw a full-page color ad in your favorite magazine telling you to eat fresh beets? Have you ever seen a TV commercial pushing raw carrots?

It only pays to run full-page ads for canned or frozen peas produced by a tall, obviously mentally retarded young fellow who tramps through the pea fields guffawing as he tramples his sponsor's product. Maybe he knows something we don't know.

Anyhow, fresh raw vegetables can be worked into a family diet very nicely if they are served in salads. Incidentally, *raw* is a key word. With rare exceptions, vegetables are *not* improved nutritionally by cooking them. Fresh vegetables contain valuable enzymes—in addition to vitamins and minerals—which are extremely useful in maintaining good health. Cooking destroys them. We've all read the injunctions to save the cooking water—but you never have to have any in the first place if you eat your high-fiber vegetables raw. A tiny word of caution. There are a very few vegetables that you shouldn't eat raw. Rhubarb, spinach, cranberries, and parsley—in large quantities—can give you enough oxalic acid to make trouble in some cases. Never eat vegetables such as manioc, malanga, or yucca raw—they contain inconvenient amounts of cyanide. Don't laugh—in major U.S. cities all these "exotics" can be found in the produce department— just know what you're eating.

All vegetables in these salads can be eaten raw in any rational amount. (If you want to eat a pound of cucumbers, that's beyond us.) But all these recipes have been tested on hearty eaters, and there is no hazard of overdosing on julienned carrots.

A word or two about dressings. Most of the dressings are included in the recipes—if you want to make your own, that's fine. But don't be a sucker and buy those heavily touted commercial salad dressings in those precious little bottles. They are fabulously expensive—about five dollars a gallon and up, which is a lot to pay for the exciting ingredients. Those ingredients include things like tap water, disodium-ethylene-diamine-tetracetate, sodium carboxymethylcellulose, and dioctyl-sodium-sulfosuccinate. If you want to save the five dollars and have a vegetable salad instead of a chemical salad, make your own dressing and spend what you save on something that will bring you pleasure instead of pain.

A final note. It would be much better if you could raise your own lettuce and cabbage and onions and everything else for these salads. If you can, do it. But if you can't, there is still hope. You can grow your own bean sprouts. They are fast, simple to grow, eminently tasty, and contain fabulous amounts of vitamins and other good things. For example, the amount of niacin in mung beans—the traditional "Chinese" bean sprouts—increases 400 percent if you simply sprout the beans. The amount of vitamin C in soybeans shoots up five and a half times as they are sprouted.

Recipes

I love this salad! And so will you—provided, of course, that you love avocados and onions. But the texture, flavor, and piquancy are unsurpassed for aficionados of the king of vegetables and the queen of fruits.

Avocado-Onion Salad—Traditional

SERVING TIME: 10 MINUTES

5 avocados, cubed
2 medium sweet onions, sliced thin
1 large green pepper, chopped fine
4 tbsps. olive **or** salad oil

3 tbsps. wine vinegar **or** lemon juice
Freshly ground black pepper
2 cloves garlic, minced
2 cups shredded lettuce

Put the avocados, onions, and green peppers into a salad bowl along with an avocado seed. The seed will keep the avocado from turning brown. Toss the ingredients with the oil and vinegar or lemon juice, pepper, and garlic. Serve on a bed of shredded lettuce. Serves 6.

🝊 🝖

Fresh! Fresh! Fresh! This salad, above all, has to be fresh! Beautiful crisp lettuce from the garden, picked early in the morning. Plump *fresh* mushrooms with that creamy white skin. Chill the lettuce, make the dressing moments before, and then put everything together. You can then use this as the standard comparison for all other salads.

Lettuce and Mushroom Salad—Traditional

SERVING TIME: 15 MINUTES

1 large head of iceberg lettuce
or *2 medium heads of*
romaine lettuce
1 pound fresh mushrooms
2 to 3 cloves garlic, minced

1 raw egg
⅓ cup olive oil
¼ cup lemon juice
1 tsp. soy sauce
⅓ cup Parmesan cheese
Freshly ground black pepper

Wash the lettuce, dry well, and tear into bite-size pieces. Wrap lettuce in a towel and store in refrigerator until ready for use. In the meantime wash, dry, and slice mushrooms. In a blender put garlic, egg, olive oil, lemon juice, and soy sauce, and blend well. In a salad bowl put the lettuce and mushrooms. Pour over them the salad dressing. Toss. Sprinkle with Parmesan cheese and freshly ground black pepper. Toss again and serve. Serves 6.

🜲 🜳

You can almost taste all the enzymes tingling on the tip of your tongue! Not to mention the vitamins, minerals, and fiber. For a nice dressing variation, take the vinegar and spices, add an egg, and blend for about a minute in your blender.

Fresh Mixed Garden Salad—Traditional

SERVING TIME: 15–20 MINUTES

1 pound fresh small green beans	*2 medium onions, thinly sliced*
1 small cauliflower	*3 carrots, cut julienne*
3 cloves garlic, minced	*⅓ cup olive oil*
2 medium turnips, cut julienne	*¼ cup wine vinegar*
2 medium beets, cut julienne	*1½ tbsps. marjoram*

Put a large pot of water on the stove to boil. In the meantime, wash the green beans and trim their tips. Wash and separate the cauliflower into flowerets. Then cut into smaller bite-size pieces. When the water is boiling well, put in the green beans, and after the water comes to a boil again, let the green beans cook about 5 minutes. They should still have the crunch in them. DO NOT COOK THE OTHER VEGETABLES. They don't need to be cooked, and if you've never tried them raw, you'll be in for a deliciously delightful surprise. Drain the beans and cool. In a large salad bowl put minced garlic with the rest of the vegetables. Sprinkle over the olive oil, vinegar, and marjoram, and toss. Serves 6.

freshly ground pepper, and toss with the salad oil and wine vinegar. Serves 6.

🐦 🐦

This is coleslaw—but like you've never tasted it before. This time it has "cilantro"! Cilantro is the leaves of coriander plant— the same one that brings you the ground coriander that comes in little boxes on the supermarket shelves. But most desirable are the fresh green leaves, which have a fresh tangy mellow chartreuse flavor. (Try it in this salad, and then see if you can define it any more precisely than we did.) It also masquerades under the name of "Chinese parsley"—justly—and is called "culantro" outside of Mexico. (The Mexicans take exception to the slightly naughty pun implicit in that form of the word.)

Coleslaw—Traditional

SERVING TIME: 15 MINUTES

1 medium head of cabbage
3 sweet green or red peppers,
  sliced thin
2 medium onions, sliced thin
2 tomatoes
3–4 sprigs of cilantro (also
  called Chinese parsley, the
  leaves of the coriander
  plant) or 2 tsp. ground
  coriander and 2 tsp. chervil

Freshly ground black pepper,
  to taste
¼–⅓ cup olive oil or other
  salad oil
¼ cup wine vinegar

Finely slice the cabbage. Thinly slice the green peppers, onions, and tomatoes and mince the cilantro. (The cilantro can be purchased in most supermarkets and in Chinese grocery stores. It is so delicious, it is worth looking for or growing in a herb pot in the kitchen.) Sprinkle with freshly ground pepper, toss everything together with the oil and vinegar, and serve. Serves 6.

🌿🌿

By now I'm sure you're familiar with the skin problems of cucumbers. Produce people just love to dip them in vats of wax, but eating wax is hazardous to your health. So unwax those cukes with soap, hot water, and a brush. You can tell when they're fit to eat by scraping the cucumber with the flat side of a knife blade. If you don't pile up a little hill of wax, it's ready to eat.

Cucumber Salad—Traditional

SERVING TIME: 10 MINUTES

4 cucumbers, thinly sliced
  with skin (wash skin well
  with hot water and soap to
  remove wax)
1 sweet Spanish onion, thinly
  sliced

2 medium green or red sweet
  peppers, thinly sliced
2 tbsps. oil
¼ cup wine vinegar
2 tbsps. honey

Mix all the ingredients before you prepare dinner so that the flavors can be blending in the refrigerator. Serve on lettuce leaves. Serves 6.

🌿🌿

Cucumbers love to swim in yogurt. Give them a chance and you'll see what we mean—they just glide around like happy little dolphins. Make sure this gets to the table icy cold.

Cucumber and Yogurt Salad—Traditional

SERVING TIME: 10 MINUTES

6 *small- to medium-size
  cucumbers, with skin (wash
  the cucumbers well with
  warm water and soap to
  remove wax)*
3 *cloves garlic, minced*
1½ *cups yogurt*

1½ *tbsps. crushed dried mint
  (or better yet, ¼ cup fresh
  mint, chopped)*
1 *medium onion, sliced thin
  (optional, for those who love
  onion in everything)*

Slice the cucumbers very thin—you can use the slicer side of your grater effectively. Mix in a salad bowl the minced garlic, cucumbers, yogurt, mint and onion (if desired), and chill thoroughly. Serves 6.

🌀🌀

American eggplant—the big globular variety—unfortunately has a tendency to be bitter. There are two alternatives: find the long slender "Armenian" or "Oriental" eggplant and use it, or simply soak the supermarket eggplant in salt water for half an hour. Please don't neglect this step—it makes a big difference. This raw salad is high fiber, full of the natural goodness of uncooked vegetables, and it tastes divine.

Raw Eggplant Salad—Traditional

SERVING TIME: 10 MINUTES

2 *small young eggplants,
  washed, dried, and cubed*
1 *medium onion, chopped*
2 *small green peppers,
  chopped*
2 *large tomatoes, chopped*
2 *cloves garlic, minced*

1 *tbsp. crushed dried oregano*
4 *tbsps. wine vinegar* **or** *lemon
  juice*
6 *tbsps. olive oil*
⅓ *cup Parmesan cheese*
*Freshly ground black pepper
  to taste*

Put the eggplant cubes into a large pot of cold water to which has been added 1 tablespoon salt. Let stand in the salted water, weighted down with a dish, for 30 minutes. Drain the eggplant and wash well to remove any excess salt. Dry the eggplant and put in a large salad bowl. Add the other vegetables. Mince garlic and add to salad bowl with oregano, vinegar or lemon juice, olive oil, Parmesan cheese, and freshly ground pepper to taste. Toss well and serve on lettuce leaves. Serves 6.

🔅🔅

Crisp beans are vital. Try for the longest ones and, of course, the freshest you can find. Canned beans? Impossible. Frozen beans? Not in this recipe, where "crunchy" is the name of the game.

Fresh Green Bean Salad—Traditional

SERVING TIME: 20 MINUTES

3 *pounds fresh green beans*
3 *medium onions, thinly*
 sliced
3 *large green peppers or red*
 sweet peppers, or mixed,
 thinly sliced

1 *egg*
¼ *cup olive oil*
¼ *cup lemon juice*
2 *cloves garlic, minced*
¼ *tsp. dry mustard*
 Freshly ground black pepper
 to taste

Put a large pot of water on to boil. In the meantime, wash the green beans and cut off their tips. Prepare the onions and green peppers. When the water is boiling, put in the green beans, and when the water comes to a boil again, let them cook for about 5 minutes—enough to soften them but not enough to take away the crunchiness. Drain the water and cool the beans. In a blender, add the egg, olive oil, lemon juice, garlic, and mustard. Blend well. In a salad bowl place the cooled green beans with the onions and green peppers. Pour over the dressing, and sprinkle freshly ground pepper to taste. Serves 6–8.

🔥🔥

When I was struggling to pay my way through medical school, I could never figure out why people would pay—in those days— thirty-nine cents for a pound of beans in a can, when you could buy the dry beans for six cents a pound—also in those days. Now I still can't figure out why folks use canned beans—especially now when things are tougher for everybody. Besides, the canned beans have had the flavor stewed out of them and you have to pay for a lot of things you can't even eat—like the can, the label, and the weirdo advertising. Oh, yes. Plaki is a Middle Eastern stand-by. Easy to make, nutritious, full of fiber, and improves day by day— if there's ever any left over.

Plaki or Cold Bean Salad—Traditional

SERVING TIME: 15 MINUTES

½ cup northern beans
4 cups water
4 carrots, cubed
1 pound potatoes, cubed
1 sweet Spanish onion, thinly
   sliced
2 medium green peppers,
   chopped

2 cloves garlic, minced
¼ cup chopped parsley
¼ cup lemon juice **or** wine
   vinegar
¼ cup olive oil
4 ounces tomato sauce
Freshly ground black pepper
   to taste

Rinse the beans and cook in the water about one hour. Add cubed carrots and potatoes and cook 10 minutes more. Drain and mix with the rest of the ingredients. Chill and serve. Serves 6.

🔥🔥

Use fresh new potatoes and be sure to wash the capers to get the salt out of them. Remember that the capers are optional and you can leave them out if you prefer since fresh capers are hard to find—to say the least. But here's a fascinating idea. If you grow your own nasturtiums, you can chop up a few of the leaves and add them to this salad for a wonderful flavor. You can also garnish the salad with nasturtium flowers. Why, you'll be the only one on your block!

Garden Potato Salad—Traditional

SERVING TIME: 15–20 MINUTES

2 *pounds (6–8) potatoes*
1 *cup chopped green onions*
¼ *cup chopped or sliced radishes*
2 *green peppers, chopped or sliced*
6 *hard-boiled eggs, sliced*
1 *cup chopped celery with leaves*

1 *medium cucumber, scrubbed and diced (with skin)*
2 *tbsps. fresh capers (optional)*
⅓ *cup lemon juice* **or** *wine vinegar*
⅓ *cup olive oil*
Freshly ground black pepper, to taste
¼ *cup chopped fresh parsley*
1 *tbsp. crushed rosemary*

Scrub and boil potatoes. Slice them, leaving on the skin. In a large salad bowl, toss potatoes with the rest of the ingredients. Serve warm or cold. Serves 6–8.

Variation:
Use mayonnaise (see Chapter 15) instead of lemon juice or wine vinegar and oil. Substitute 1 tablespoon tarragon for rosemary.

🌀🌀

This Japanese-style salad has unexpected ingredients, but they all live together in absolute harmony. Everything should be nice and cold, although not necessarily icy. You'll enjoy it.

Sweet and Sour Rice Salad—Traditional

SERVING TIME: 15 MINUTES

3¾ cups water
¼ cup vinegar
2 cups washed brown rice
1 medium cucumber, diced
1 bunch radishes, diced

2 medium green peppers,
minced
6 green onions, finely chopped
1 raw beet, diced

In a 2½–3-quart saucepan bring water and vinegar to a boil. Add rice. When rice begins to boil again, lower heat, cover, and simmer for 40 minutes. Chill. In the meantime prepare vegetables. Toss the vegetables and chilled rice with the following dressing:

¼ cup oil
¼ cup vinegar

¼ cup honey

Serves 6.

Quick and Easy (SERVING TIME: 10 MINUTES)
Prepare the rice ahead of time with the vinegar water or use rice already cooked in any other way. Prepare the vegetables and toss with the dressing, adding extra dressing for extra flavor, if necessary.

Super-Instant (SERVING TIME: 5 MINUTES)
Prepare the rice ahead of time. Prepare the vegetables ahead of time. All you have to do is toss and serve.

Bran Supplement: ½ cup bran with extra dressing if needed.

Sarma is often used as the filling for rolled grape leaves. You can do it that way if you like, but that means getting fresh tender grape leaves from a friend, boiling them to soften them up, filling them with raw Sarma, and then cooking the mixture. Don't use canned or bottled grape leaves—they are chemically treated. And besides, this recipe gives 90 percent of pleasure of the more complex version.

Sarma—Traditional

- -

SERVING TIME: 20 MINUTES

6 *onions, chopped*
1 *cup olive oil*
1 *cup brown rice, washed*
⅓ *cup minced parsley*
¼ *cup minced fresh dill*
1 *tsp. allspice*
1 *tsp. cinnamon*
1 *tsp. paprika*
1 *tsp. chili powder*

¼–½ *tsp. ground chili (hot New Mexico)*
½ *tsp. freshly ground black pepper*
1 *cup water*
⅓ *cup currants*
⅓ *cup pignolias*
Juice of 1 lemon

In a large frying pan sauté chopped onions in the olive oil until transparent. Add the washed rice and all the herbs and spices, water, currants, nuts, and lemon juice. Cover and simmer about 40 minutes, or until the rice is cooked. Chill. Mound on a platter and serve with wedges of lemon. Serves 4–6.

Variation:
Add 1 large can of whole mussels and cook with the rice mixture the 40 minutes. Chill and serve.

🌶️ 🌶️

This nifty salad is a cousin to the Mexican and Latin American classic known as *pico de gallo*, or "beak of the rooster." (I'd love to explain *all* those names but if I did there wouldn't be any room for recipes. And eating is a lot more fun than ctymology. So I'll just slip in a few once in a while.) Don't tell your husband, "Dear, we're going to have onion and orange salad for dinner tonight." Just serve it and things will be fine.

Orange Onion Salad—Traditional

SERVING TIME: 15 MINUTES

6 large oranges
2 medium onions
Juice of 3 lemons

1½–3 tsps. ground chili or
chili powder; ground chili is
better, really

Peel and slice the oranges or break into sections. Thinly slice the
onions. Salad plates can be attractively arranged individually and
each one sprinkled with the juice of half a lemon and ¼ to ½
teaspoon of the ground chili. The ground chili is a little piquant,
and you may want each individual to sprinkle to his own taste.
But this makes a refreshing salad, especially as an accompaniment
to a pork or duck roast.

🐚🦀

All you slaves to canned fruit salad—throw off your chains!
Say good-bye to poison-packed iridescent maraschino cherries
and pale-green embalmed grapes. Say hello to real fruit flavor—
as the food company ads say when they mean a can full of
chemicals. But this salad has real fruit—you can't do any better.
And it's just as easy to make in December as it was in June,
except for June we have a Summer Fruit Salad for you!

Fresh Winter Fruit Salad—Traditional

SERVING TIME: 15–20 MINUTES

6 large oranges, peeled and
sectioned
6 grapefruits, peeled and
sectioned
6 apples, scrubbed and sliced

3 bananas, sliced and
sprinkled with lemon juice
Honey to taste, if necessary
1 cup nuts, optional

In a large salad bowl toss the fruits and add honey if desired.
Serve on lettuce leaves or in deep fruit bowls. Serves 6–8.

Variation:

Add 1 cup chopped celery and 1 onion, chopped, to the above and serve with the following dressing: ¼ cup lemon juice, ¼–⅓ cup olive oil, ¼ cup chopped fresh mint, or 1 tablespoon crushed dried mint, 1 teaspoon ground chili, or to taste.

🌀🌀

Lovely, lovely, lovely! Sweet, crisp, tart, crunchy, mouth-watering! You couldn't do any better. Wash your fruit well—don't be afraid to use soap on the skins if you have any doubts —cool it, but don't ice it, and you'll be delighted. Expensive to make? But isn't that what money is for—to increase your sensual pleasure, protect your health, and make life more exciting?

Fresh Summer Fruit Salad—Traditional

SERVING TIME: 20–30 MINUTES

2 *cups canteloupe balls, or diced*
2 *cups honeydew balls, or diced*
1 *fresh pineapple, cored, peeled, and diced*
2 *cups sliced fresh peaches*
1 *cup sliced fresh apricots*
4 *large oranges, peeled and sectioned*
1 *cup blueberries*
2 *cups diced and seeded watermelon*
2–3 *tangerines, peeled and sectioned*

1 *bunch grapes*
1 *cup cherries*
2 *cups sliced nectarines*
2 *mangoes, diced (optional)*
1 *small papaya, diced (optional)*
3 *bananas, sliced in rounds and sprinkled with lemon juice*
Juice of 1 orange
Juice of 1 lemon
Honey, to taste, if necessary
1 *cup nuts (optional)*

In a large salad bowl mix and blend the fruits, juices, and honey. Serve in deep fruit bowls or on beds of lettuce. Serves 6–8.

13

Desserts

Strangely enough, desserts are the least important chapter of *The Save-Your-Life-Diet High-Fiber Cookbook*. This is the reason: once you really get going on a full-fledged high-fiber diet, your interest in sweets will begin to decline. So often people find the traditional low-fiber American diet unsatisfying and unfulfilling. The irresistible temptation is to use dessert to pack all those empty spaces—the physical ones and the emotional ones as well.

The high-fiber diet is fulfilling—both physically, because of the nature of fiber, and emotionally. There is something good and natural about consuming the diet that has sustained the human race for at least 50,000 years. There is something sadly lacking *emotionally* in a diet composed of Jello, Cool-Whip, frozen dinners, nitrated sausage, imitation "bread," imitation "butter," and chemical-laden "breakfast cereals."

In the United States, most food is dosed with refined sugar to blunt the eater's taste mechanism and disguise the inferior flavor of the manufactured product. This sin is most evident in desserts. We try to atone for this by featuring desserts rich in fiber and totally devoid of refined sugar. Some of these desserts include chocolate, which deserves a few words in its defense.

Most "chocolate" sold in this country simply isn't *chocolate*. That bar of "milk chocolate," for example, may contain as little as *10* percent chocolate, plus exciting things like cereal extract, mono- and diglycerides, sorbitan monostearate, polysorbate 60, powdered skim milk, dried corn syrup, and above all, lecithin. Lecithin is only there to fool you. By adding this cheap soybean extract in the insignificant amount of *three-tenths of 1 percent*, the "chocolate" manufacturers can steal 4 percent of the very expensive cocoa butter from the final product. Cocoa butter costs more than any other prime material in the manufacture of chocolate. Now, there's nothing wrong with lecithin, but remember you're paying big money for a "chocolate" bar, not a chocolate-flavored lecithin-spiked, skim-milk-laden chemical cocktail. Besides that, it has become fashionable in certain circles to condemn chocolate and praise carob. There's nothing wrong with carob—except it's rather expensive. But there's nothing wrong with chocolate if you mean real chocolate—the pure product of the bean of the cacao tree. Probably the best kind of chocolate to use is unsweetened cooking or baking chocolate. This *should* be nothing more than the solidified form of the chocolate liquor produced by cleaning and melting the cocoa bean. This delicious dark solid is relatively high in fiber and vegetable fat. You can add your own sweetening in the form of honey or molasses. You don't have to add lecithin or things like sorbitan monostearate—unless you have some tremendous craving for them. We hope you like these desserts, but you won't hurt our feelings if you simply opt for a nice piece of fresh fruit to top off your high-fiber meal.

Recipes

Try to use pippin apples, russets, or Jonathans. Stay away from the supermarket specials, those big mushy monstrosities known as "cooking apples," presumably because they're not good to eat. Try to get whole nutmeg and grind it yourself in the blender just before using.

Apple Crisp—Traditional

SERVING TIME: 10–15 MINUTES

6 cups sliced apples
½–⅔ cup honey, depending
  on tartness of apples
1½ tbsps. cinnamon

¾ tsp. nutmeg
½ cup whole-wheat pastry
  flour
4 tbsps. butter

Spread the apples in an 8- or 9-inch square pan or casserole which has been greased. Pour the honey over the apples and sprinkle them with 1 tablespoon cinnamon and ½ teaspoon nutmeg. Toss the apples and spices, mixing well. In a bowl mix the flour, butter, ½ tablespoon cinnamon and ¼ teaspoon nutmeg, working the mixture with your fingers until it looks like pea-size crumbs. Sprinkle this crumbly mixture over the top of the apples. Bake in preheated 350-degree oven for 50–60 minutes until apples are tender and the top a golden brown. Serve with whipped cream or ice cream. Serves 6.

Variation:
For the topping mix ½ cup honey with 4 tablespoons butter, 1½ tablespoons cinnamon, ¾ teaspoon nutmeg and ½ cup rolled oats.

🦞🦐

Simple, unadorned, pristine—an American classic. Use good crisp, tart apples, as in the Apple Crisp. Grind the cinnamon just before using.

Old-Fashioned Apple Pie—Traditional

SERVING TIME: 15–20 MINUTES

Pie Crust:
1 recipe High-Fiber Pie   1 egg white
    Dough (p. 66)

Filling:
6 cups sliced apples   3–4 tbsps. cinnamon
½–1 cup honey, depending on   1–2 tbsps. ginger (optional, for
    how tart the apples are   a slight change in flavor)

Line the bottom of a 9-inch pie plate with half the dough. Brush this bottom piece with egg white. This keeps the bottom crust from becoming soggy. Begin to layer the apples, sprinkling some of the honey and cinnamon over each layer of apples until you've used all the apples. Wet the edges of the bottom crust. Cover with the other half of the dough, and seal the edges by pressing around the edge with the tines of a fork. Cut a couple of slits in the top crust. Brush top crust with milk or beaten egg. Bake in preheated 450-degree oven for 10 minutes. Lower heat to 350 degrees and bake 30 to 40 minutes.

When you eat *this* pecan pie you will be eating pecan pie for the first time in your life. This is absolutely true. All other versions include such insults to your intelligence—and taste buds —as corn syrup, refined white sugar, refined white flour, and margarine. Be sure to use good fresh *unfried* pecans—and unsalted if you can find them. Pecan pie should be a wild untamed dish—dark and mysterious. Try this recipe and you'll see what we mean . . .

Pecan Pie—Traditional

SERVING TIME: 10 MINUTES

½ recipe High-Fiber Pie Dough (p.66)
Filling:
¼ cup butter   *3 eggs*
½ cup honey   *1 tsp. vanilla*
½ cup pure maple syrup   *2 cups pecan halves*

Cream butter with honey and maple syrup. Add eggs, vanilla, and pecans. Blend well. Pour this filling into an 8-inch pie plate that has been lined with the pastry dough. Bake in preheated 350-degree oven about 20 minutes, or until an inserted knife comes out clean. Serves 6–8.

Bread pudding made with real bread is wonderful. A flavored mush made with imitation white "bread" is, well, let's say, not quite the same. Try it and you'll see.

Grandmother's Bread Pudding—Traditional

SERVING TIME: 10–15 MINUTES

4 cups milk
2 tbsps. butter
½ cup honey
4 eggs
3 cups whole-wheat bread
  cubes

½ cup bran
½ cup raisins
1 cup chopped nuts
1 tbsp. cinnamon
½ tsp. nutmeg
1 tsp. vanilla

Scald the milk. Add the butter and honey. While the milk-butter mixture is cooling a bit, in another bowl beat the eggs. Gradually add the eggs to the milk-butter mixture while beating with a wire whisk. Stir in the bread cubes, bran, raisins, nuts, cinnamon, nutmeg, and vanilla. Pour into a 2½–3-quart baking dish. Bake in a preheated 350-degree oven 50–60 minutes. Serves 6.

Bundt Cake—Traditional

SERVING TIME: 7–10 MINUTES

1 cup butter
1½ cups honey
8 eggs
1 tsp. vanilla

Juice of a lemon and grated
  rind of lemon or juice of an
  orange and grated rind of
  half an orange
4 tsps. baking powder
4 cups whole-wheat pastry
  flour (approx.)*

* Depending on the size of your eggs and whether you use the lemon juice or orange juice, the amount of flour varies. You don't want too stiff a cake dough, so begin with 3 cups and work your way up. The dough should pour into the bundt pan.

Preheat oven to 350 degrees. Cream the butter and honey well. Add the eggs one by one, beating after each addition. If at this point the mixture doesn't seem to blend, don't worry. The final result will be perfect. Add the vanilla, the juice of the lemon or orange, the rind, and the baking powder, and while the mixer is mixing, gradually add the flour, putting in up to 3 cups to begin with and adding by half cups until you have a moist but not too stiff cake dough. Grease an 8–10-cup bundt cake mold or a 9 x 3-inch angel-food pan, then lightly flour it and pour in the cake batter. Bake for 40–50 minutes. It's a good idea at 40 minutes to pierce the cake to the bottom with a sharp knife. If the knife comes out clean, the cake is done. If not, set your timer for another 5 minutes and check again. You don't want to overbake the cake. When the cake is done, remove from bundt pan by turning it over onto a serving plate. Cool.

Variations:
• Instead of lemon or orange juice and rind, use 3 ounces of melted unsweetened chocolate.
• Add 2 tablespoons cinnamon, 1 tablespoon ginger, ¼ teaspoon cloves, and ½ teaspoon nutmeg to above.

One precaution, regrettably necessary. Use a green-skinned orange in this recipe. Many orange-colored oranges are colored with toxic dyes; if you cook with the peel, you get the poison. Green-skinned oranges can be just as ripe—the color really depends on weather conditions as much as anything else. So ripe green-colored oranges are your best bet. This is a nice simple, very light dessert. You'll find yourself serving it often.

🜚 🜛

If you compare this with those awful disgusting "gingerbread mixes," you will understand in a flash what has happened to American cooking in the past fifty years. When you taste your own gingerbread, you'll be delighted to realize that it doesn't have to happen in your house.

Old-Fashioned Gingerbread Cake—Traditional

SERVING TIME: 10 MINUTES

1 cup butter
1½ cups honey, or half honey and half molasses
3 eggs
4 tsps. baking powder
1 tsp. baking soda
1 tbsp. ground ginger
1 tsp. nutmeg
½ tsp. cloves

1 tbsp. cinnamon
1 tbsp. instant coffee
⅓ cup cocoa or 2 squares unsweetened chocolate, melted
1 tsp. vanilla
4¼ cups whole-wheat pastry flour
1¾ cups water

In a mixing bowl cream the butter. Add the honey or honey and molasses and cream with the butter. Add the eggs one by one, beating after each addition. Add baking powder, baking soda, spices, instant coffee, cocoa or melted chocolate, and vanilla. Beat. Add flour and water alternately, beating well. Pour into greased 13 × 9 × 2 baking pan and bake in preheated 350-degree oven for 20–30 minutes. DO NOT OVERBAKE. After 20 minutes test the cake with a toothpick. If the toothpick does not come out clean, set your timer for another 5 minutes. Check again. Serve with whipped cream which has been whipped with 2 tablespoons honey and 1 teaspoon vanilla. Serves 8.

🦐🦐

This is not a dish to crank out every night, but on the other hand, you don't have to make it very often because it will linger in your memory for months. Use good vanilla—imported from Latin America if possible—for the best flavor. Major-brand vanilla tends to have a chemical-laboratory flavor (and not by accident). You'll be very happy with this dessert. Resist the temptation to serve it *instead* of a meal.

Chocolate-Fruit Fondue—Traditional

SERVING TIME: 20–25 MINUTES

3 tbsps. butter
8 ounces unsweetened
   chocolate
1 cup milk
Platter of:
Fresh pineapple chunks
Sliced fresh pears
Sliced bananas
Grapes

2 cups honey
2 tsps. vanilla
2 cups chopped walnuts or
   pecans (optional)

Sliced apples
Sliced fresh peaches
Sliced fresh nectarines
Cherries

Arrange your own favorite combination on a large platter.

In a saucepan melt the butter and chocolate. Stir in the milk gradually. Add the honey and boil the mixture until it reaches the soft-ball stage, which is about 236° on the thermometer. Remove from heat. Add the vanilla and nuts, if desired. Pour into a fondue pot which is set over a warmer. Each person can dip his selection of fruits into the chocolate. Serves 6.

🦋🦋

This is an extravaganza suitable for the most special of all special occasions. It is the most sensational of all high-fiber desserts—and may be the most sensational of all desserts. It is very easy to make, but, by the time you've been through this book you will have gotten over that television-commercial complex of thinking that time spent cooking is time wasted. Is it more important to polish the vinyl-asbestos tile on the floor until you can see the sponsor's product reflected in it or is it more rewarding to prepare good wholesome food that improves your health and brightens your life? You be the judge.

Viennese Fruit Creme—Traditional

SERVING TIME: 20–25 MINUTES

*1 cup sliced bananas sprinkled
with lemon juice
1 cup sliced fresh pears,
sprinkled with lemon juice
1 cup pitted fresh cherries
1 cup diced fresh pineapple
1 cup seedless grapes
1 cup sliced fresh peaches,
sprinkled with lemon juice*

*1 cup sliced fresh nectarines,
sprinkled with lemon juice
1 cup diced fresh mango
(optional)
1 pound strawberry jam
1 pint heavy cream, whipped
8 ounces unsweetened
chocolate
1 cup honey*

In a 3-quart serving bowl put all the fruit and toss well. Mix the jam into the whipped cream and spread the jam-cream mixture on top of the fruit. In a medium frying pan melt the chocolate over low heat being careful not to burn it. Add the honey and let it boil for 5 minutes. Cool the chocolate. Pour the cooled chocolate over the jam-whipped cream, carefully covering it completely. Chill. Serves 6–8.

Fast, easy, and fun. You can show the kids how to make them in a jiffy. And you can let them eat these fine cookies without worrying.

High-Fiber Refrigerator Cookies—Traditional

SERVING TIME: 7–10 MINUTES

*1 cup butter
1 cup honey
2 eggs
3 tsps. vanilla*

*1 tsp. baking soda
3¾–4 cups whole-wheat
pastry **or** stone-ground
whole-wheat flour*

In the mixing bowl cream the butter and honey. Add the eggs and beat. Add vanilla, baking soda, and flour, slowly at first, then quickly, to blend everything well. Cut two sheets of wax paper and put half the dough on each sheet. Shape the dough into log shapes, using the wax paper to help you shape. Wrap the wax paper around the logs and chill the dough at least one hour. If you're in a hurry, put the log shapes into the freezer for about 10 minutes. The idea is to chill the dough enough so that it will be easy to slice. Slice the cookies about ⅛ to ¼ inch in width. Place them on a greased cookie sheet and bake in preheated 350-degree oven for 8–10 minutes. Makes 6–8 dozen, depending on the size of your cookie.

Variations:
· *Chocolate:* Add ¼ cup of cocoa or 2 squares melted unsweetened chocolate. If you add cocoa, you might reduce the flour by ¼ cup. If you use the melted chocolate, you might need just a bit more flour to make a stiff dough.
· *Spice:* Add 2 heaping tablespoons of ground cinnamon, 1 tablespoon ground ginger, ¼ teaspoon cloves, and ½ teaspoon nutmeg.
· *Nuts:* Add 1–1½ cups of finely chopped nuts to any of the above.

Bunuelos (pronounced "bun-weigh-lows") are sold in the streets, on the beaches, in the parks—everywhere in Latin America. They are about as good as anything can be. They are distinctly high fiber, contain substantial amounts of protein and vitamins. Everybody in your family will like them. Make plenty.

Bunuelos—Traditional

SERVING TIME: 30–40 MINUTES

2 cups stone-ground whole-
  wheat flour
1 tbsp. honey
2 tsps. baking powder
2 eggs

1 tsp. vanilla
2 tbsps. melted butter
¼–½ cup milk
Oil for frying

On a board put the flour. Make a well in the center and add the honey, baking powder, and eggs. Begin to work the liquid into the flour. Add vanilla and butter and as much milk as you need to make a soft, unsticky dough. Knead the dough a few minutes. Divide the dough into 12 1-inch balls. On a lightly floured cloth or board roll out each ball to the size of a tortilla. In a large frying pan heat the oil to 365 degrees. Use a candy thermometer to be sure that you don't go beyond 370 degrees. Fry each bunuelo until it is a light golden brown on each side. Drain the bunuelos on paper toweling. Glaze them with the following:

Glaze:
1 cup honey

¼ cup water

1 tbsp. cinnamon

1 tbsp. butter

Put the above ingredients into a saucepan. Heat until boiling. Boil a few minutes until a drop of the syrup dropped into cold water forms a firm ball which can be flattened when taken out of the water. This is between 245 and 250 on the candy thermometer. Spoon this glaze over the drained bunuelos and put them on a rack to cool. They will be a little sticky but yummy. If you have time, you might even put them into the freezer to harden the glaze. Makes about a dozen bunuelos.

14
Candy

People who eat truly high-fiber diets don't usually have much taste for candy. It works the same as desserts. If you go around half-starved all day you have to assuage your hunger with something—and you fall victim to candy bars and other indescribably bad things to put into your mouth.

Candy bars—and much of commercially made candy in the United States these days—have an interesting story behind them. The increased consumption of commercial candy in the United States is making soap very expensive in Latin America. Hard to understand? Tragically, it's simple and it works this way:

For decades in Central and South America—and Mexico—soap was made by boiling coconut oil with lye in gigantic vats. The soap was cheap, lathered magnificently, and had a good feel. However, in recent years American candy manufacturers have come into the market and are buying this important soap ingredient to sell for human consumption. They flavor it with artificial flavors (of course), add artificial coloring (of course), pack it in brightly colored wrappers (of course), and advertise it intensely (of course). What Latins used to do the laundry with, Americans are eating during their "candy break." Coconut oil has one other little problem: It is the greatest source of the fearsome "saturated fats" that are believed by the cholesterol theorists to cause heart attacks. Millions of American kids are eating "corn oil margarine" instead of pure butter and stuffing their little tummies with a fat that is among the most cholesterol producing. Isn't that interesting?

These nice candies all contain dietary fiber and we think you'll like them.

Recipes

You'll like this—and so will everyone else. It's so good for you that it's really not fair to classify it as candy. But it's so good to eat that we couldn't think of any other place to put it.

Sesame Seed Candy—Traditional

SERVING TIME: 10–15 MINUTES

2 cups sesame seeds
2 cups honey

1 tbsp. lemon juice

Toast the sesame seeds in a large frying pan over medium to high heat, stirring frequently. This will only take a few minutes. In a large saucepan combine the toasted sesame seeds with the honey and lemon juice. Heat to boiling and boil until the temperature reaches 280–290 degrees on the candy thermometer for a chewy bar—or up to 300 degrees for brittle. Spread on a greased pan and let cool.

Any relation between this delicious candy and commercial halvah is impossible. This one is made from a ten-thousand-year-old recipe. When you try some, you'll see why it has endured so long.

Halvah—Traditional

SERVING TIME: 5 MINUTES

1½ cups unhulled sesame
   seeds
4 tbsps. honey

2 tsps. vanilla
A few drops of sesame oil, if
   needed

In a blender, at high speed, begin blending the sesame seeds. If they don't seem to have enough oil to make a paste, add a drop or two at a time until the blended seeds form a pasty mass. Stop blender frequently and stir with rubber bottle spatula. Add honey and vanilla and blend some more. Form the halvah into balls or press into a square pan. Chill. When chilled, the halvah in the pan can be cut into bite-size squares. This is not only good as a candy, but also as a spread. I used to eat this on toast in the morning when I was little. Makes about 1 cup paste.

Variation:
· Add 2 teaspoons cocoa or ½ square of unsweetened chocolate, melted, to the above recipe.

Use unsalted, unfried, and preferably raw nuts for this one. It will last—from the moment it cools until it is eaten—about one minute and thirty seconds. At least that's the record in our house.

Nut Brittle—Traditional

SERVING TIME: 10–15 MINUTES

2 cups honey
¼ cup water
2 tbsps. butter

1 tsp. vanilla
2 cups nuts (any one, or a combination)

In a deep saucepan combine honey, water, and butter. Bring to a boil and let boil until it reaches 300 degrees on the candy thermometer. When the syrup is dropped into cold water it breaks up into hard, brittle threads. Watch carefully to be sure syrup does not boil over. Remove from the heat. Add the vanilla and nuts and spread on a greased cookie sheet or foil pan to cool. Break into pieces and serve.

🔥🔥

Sweet—in a good way. A nice source of protein. A good dose of fiber. Put it all together and you get what we want you to enjoy: guilt-free candy for you and your kids.

Pecan Penuche—Traditional

SERVING TIME: 5–7 MINUTES

2 cups honey
¾ cup milk or cream
1 tbsp. butter

1 tsp. vanilla
1½ cups pecans

In a heavy saucepan combine honey, milk or cream, and butter. Cook, stirring, over medium heat until well blended and butter is melted. Continue to cook until the syrup reaches the soft-ball stage—which is 240 degrees on the candy thermometer. Remove the candy from the heat and let cool to about 110 degrees on the candy thermometer. Add vanilla, and with a wooden spoon beat the candy until it becomes thick and creamy. Add the nuts. Pour into a greased square baking pan and cool. Cut into squares and serve.

🔥🔥

From Cuba we have this charming version of a "jawbreaker." The unsweetened chocolate is the source of fiber and it's something nice to serve to guests.

Rompe-quejada—Traditional

SERVING TIME: 5–7 MINUTES

3 squares unsweetened
   chocolate
2 tbsps. butter
½ cup milk

¾–1 cup honey (depending
   on whether you want these
   to be bittersweet or
   normally sweet)
2 tsps. vanilla

In a heavy saucepan melt the chocolate and butter. Gradually add the milk, blending well. Add honey and boil with syrup for 5–7 minutes until a drop of syrup dropped in a glass of cold water becomes hard but not brittle. This is about 265° on the candy thermometer and should take about half an hour. Stir in vanilla. Grease a sheet of wax paper. Drop the rompe-quejada by spoonfuls onto the greased wax paper. When cool, these have the consistency of a hard caramel. Makes about 30 candies.

15
A Few Standard Recipes

There are certain items that every kitchen needs. Too many people have been duped into believing that the only place they can get these essentials is at the supermarket. Not true. You can make them better, cheaper, and more enjoyably in the privacy and sanctuary of your own kitchen. Here they are—and they'll help make every taste better—and healthier.

That store-bought mayonnaise—the kind that shouts, "Hey! I'm *really* mayonnaise!"—should also whisper something else. It should tell you: "I also might contain calcium disodium ethylene diamine tetracetate, MSG, citric acid, oxystearing, and cheapy corn syrup. But don't tell anybody, okay?" So make your own and you'll see the difference.

Mayonnaise—Traditional

SERVING TIME: 3 MINUTES

2 tbsps. lemon juice **or** vinegar   1 tsp. dry mustard
    or 1 tbsp. of each   ¼ tsp. cayenne pepper
1 cup salad oil   ¼ tsp. ground black pepper
1 egg   ¼ tsp. ground chili

In a blender put the lemon juice or vinegar, ¼ cup of the oil, egg, dry mustard, cayenne pepper, black pepper, and chili. Cover the blender jar and put at high speed. Gradually, by drops or a thin stream, add the rest of the oil through the hole in the top of the blender jar cover while the blender is blending at high speed. Makes about 1 cup.

Variation:
• *Aioli:* Add 3 to 5 cloves of garlic depending on how strong you want the aioli to be. This is delicious with anything.

Quick and Easy
Nothing could be quicker or easier than the above. However, if you're tossing a salad with an oil and vinegar dressing, break in a raw egg and toss and you will have a mayonnaise-type dressing.

🌶️ 🌶️

Don't spend good money for bad croutons. Most commercial croutons are junk "bread" fried in cheapy coconut oil. Ugh! Make your own high-fiber croutons in a flash—and you save loads of money in the process.

Croutons—Traditional

Take several thick slices of whole-wheat bread. Cut the slices into cubes. Sauté the cubes in a small amount of butter or oil until the cubes are toasted and golden in color.

Variations:
• *Garlic croutons*—Add some fresh minced garlic to the butter or oil in which you sauté the croutons.
• *Cheese croutons*—Add a few tablespoons of Parmesan to the butter or oil in which you sauté the croutons.

🌶️ 🌶️

Why should you eat yogurt? Two reasons: first, it tastes good (once you learn to appreciate it) and second, it's good for you. We won't go into all the virtues of yogurt in just a few lines, but basically it is a culture of *lactobacillus acidophilus* bacteria in milk. Regular consumption of good-quality yogurt helps this form of bacteria to predominate in your intestine instead of the kind that tends to break down bile acids into cancer-producing substances. There is also evidence that yogurt with its specific bacterial forms and acid medium helps the body defend against common intestinal infections. Some doctors who should know better have condemned yogurt—perhaps because it doesn't require a prescription. The commercial variety is usually a nutritional catastrophe—loaded with refined sugar, artificial flavoring and coloring, and packed with potentially harmful additives. Make your own, enjoy a pure healthful product with a ten-times-better taste—and spend the substantial savings on something you'd otherwise have to do without.

Yogurt—Traditional

1 quart milk   *2 tbsps. yogurt*

In a 2–2½-quart saucepan put the milk and heat to the point where it forms a skin on top—just before it begins to boil. This is 160 degrees on a candy thermometer, and is a good way to be sure that the milk gets hot enough. Carefully pour into a quart jar or deep bowl and let cool until it reads 128 degrees on the thermometer. Stir in the yogurt. Cover the jar or bowl and put into a cooler box for about 8 hours. A picnic cooler box is a good place to keep the yogurt because it keeps the temperature just right. My Grandmother used to wrap the bottle with big towels to keep in the warmth. But if you have a cooler box, the outcome is sure.

🔥🔥

Strawberry Jam—Traditional

4 cups fresh strawberries
½–1 cup honey (depending on
how sweet you like your
jam)

1 tbsp. lemon juice
2 tbsps. water
2 pieces stick cinnamon
(optional)

Wash the strawberries well. In a saucepan combine the strawberries with the honey, lemon juice, water, and cinnamon if desired. With a wooden spoon crush the berries. Bring the mixture to a boil and gently boil, stirring constantly to prevent burning, until the jam begins to thicken. The jam is done when it is thick enough to fall off the spoon in a thick mass. This is about 240 degrees on the candy thermometer. Pour into jars, cool, and store in refrigerator.

About the Authors

DR. DAVID REUBEN received his medical degree at the University of Illinois College of Medicine. He took his training in psychiatry at the Cook County Mental Health Center and served as an Air Force psychiatrist for two years, spending part of his time as a research associate at Harvard Medical School, Boston, Massachusetts. Dr. Reuben's books have sold well over eighteen million copies in twenty-five countries and have been translated into twenty-two languages.

BARBARA REUBEN received her Bachelor of Arts degree from Emerson College in Boston and her Master of Science degree from Hofstra University in New York. She is a gourmet cook, an accomplished linguist, and her husband's greatest joy.